OVERVIEW

Overview

Almost everyone has encountered difficult people in the workplace. Difficult people can exhibit different behaviors, such as rudeness, yelling, gossiping, ignoring, or harassing. Being able to deal with these people can make for a less stressful and more productive work environment.

To effectively deal with difficult people, you first need to be able to identify the type of difficult person you're dealing with. Then you can have a better understanding of the person's motivations. This will enable you to determine how best to deal with their behavior.

Identify difficult people

Difficult people can exhibit different behaviors. However, they can be categorized into a few common types. Think about some difficult people you've encountered. Perhaps someone who complained all the time. Or someone who seemed to be out only for themselves. By being able to identify the type of difficult person you're dealing with, you can better prepare a strategy to use to deal with that person.

Understand motivations

Difficult people are motivated by many things. One person might be motivated by a need for attention. Another might be motivated by a fear of failure. By understanding what motivates difficult people to act the way they do, you'll be in a better position to begin to be able to deal with them.

Deal with the behavior

In this book, you'll learn a few steps you can take to cope with the difficult behavior and do just that. Keep in mind that each person is an individual and what works for one may not work for another.

Dealing with difficult people is never pleasant. They can cause all kinds of problems and uncomfortable situations. Learning how to best deal with difficult people is a skill that will serve you well. In this book, you'll learn about some common types of difficult people and their motivations, as well as steps you can take to deal with their behavior.

Have you ever encountered someone who broke into a sudden rant? Maybe they said something like "I have never heard anything so ridiculous in my life! You're kidding me right? Why am I the only one with the intelligence to see a problem here?"

This behavior is aggressive – hostile-aggressive, to be precise – and it's one of the most difficult behaviors you'll face.

You may have also encountered the more subtle passive-aggressive behavior. Whether subtle or overt, you have to be prepared to deal with these expressions of aggression in the workplace. Hostile-aggressive and passive-aggressive behaviors are learned, and the basis of each is anger. However, each type also has its own traits.

Hostile-aggressive

Hostile-aggressive behavior is relatively easy to spot. Individuals who behave in a hostile- aggressive manner are openly angry. They'll often yell and use personal, verbal attacks to get

what they want. They're difficult to work with because their personal attacks can raise your own anger and stress levels. It's hard to stay calm and focused when you're being treated with disrespect.

Passive-aggressive

Passive-aggressive behavior is more subtle than hostile-aggressive behavior. Passive- aggressive individuals are experts at manipulation and go to great lengths to hide their true intentions. They don't show anger. Passive-aggressive behavior is hard to deal with because you never know what's really going on. You can't trust the intentions of a passive-aggressive person.

This book outlines behaviors to look for to recognize hostile-aggressive and passive-aggressive people. It also explores strategies for dealing with both when you encounter them at work.

The number one tip for dealing with hostile-aggressive types is not to take the aggressive behavior personally. A seven-step procedure that can help you deal with the incident and move forward is covered in this book.

The most important thing to remember when dealing with passive-aggressive types is that you can't change their behavior. Upon completion of this book, you should be better prepared to recognize and deal with aggressive people in your workplace.

Every workplace has someone like Nelly – someone whose negative behavior affects the harmony and efficiency of the workplace. Nelly whines that she's hard done by, she complains that others in the office aren't supporting her efforts, and worst of all, she blames coworkers for her mistakes, misunderstandings, and miscalculations.

When you have to work with difficult people like Nelly, their behavior makes it hard to relate productively to them.

They're the types who relate to others in ways that grate on the nerves and strip away the tolerance of coworkers.

Sadly, many people either just give up trying to create a positive change and settle for ignoring their difficult coworker, or they adopt negative behavior themselves.

Dealing with people is a part of life. When relationships are positive, you can reap all sorts of emotional and tangible rewards. But when you run up against negative people, it can have the opposite effect.

Why do people behave negatively at work? Often it's because negative behavior has benefited them in the past. But there are many other motivating factors:

- attempting to satisfy personal needs or agendas,
- seeking attention or validation,
- dealing with feelings of fear or inadequacy,
- relieving stress,
- displacing anger, and

- rationalizing that their own needs are more important than teamwork.

Whatever their motivation for behaving negatively, it's important to approach these difficult people proactively. Rewarding aspects of dealing with these people can be the challenge of finding a solution to their issues and establishing positive, productive work relationships.

Negative people are often described by their character types. But the terms whiner, blamer, and complainer aren't judgments about people. Rather, those descriptions relay the reactive behavior that some difficult people fall into when under stress. When you know how to deal with these types of people, you'll be able to help them move from emotional reaction to effective action.

Through this book, you'll gain practical knowledge about tools that will help you develop productive relationships with your difficult coworkers. This book covers characteristics of the types of people who demonstrate negative behavior in a work environment. It also covers the three steps for dealing with negative people, and how to use those steps to deal with three types – whiners, blamers, and complainers.

The word "manipulation" means to manage or utilize skillfully. While this can be benign – in the sense of using your hands to manipulate a machine – in the workplace it can often have an interpretation that's more difficult to deal with. Manipulators in the workplace are those people who do whatever it takes to get what they want. They control or play upon others by artful, unfair, or insidious means, making others carry out their hidden agenda.

Anyone in the workplace, from your coworker to your boss or your customer, could be a manipulative person.

Manipulative people have an arsenal of different forms of mind games to try to get what they want, maintain a grip on power, or remove something – or someone – in their way.

Manipulative people can be annoying; worse yet, they can be spiteful and malicious. Either way, their words and actions can be detrimental to your well-being, as well as to your reputation and career.

One of the worst aspects of manipulation is that people who are being manipulated often don't realize what's going on. Manipulators are subtle, and use tactics that make it seem as though they are the ones being hurt, or that they're simply being caring.

And clever manipulators exploit everyone's hidden weaknesses and insecurities. They know what emotional buttons to push to get you to do what they want without you even being aware you're being exploited.

You can't always avoid difficult people. Most people are easy enough to get along with. But there are still enough manipulative, arrogant, nosy, and annoying people in any workplace to make it impractical to simply hide in the corner and try to work in peace. These people aren't going to go away, and you can't allow them to negatively impact your interactions. You have to learn how to effectively deal with them.

Although it's human nature to be motivated by self-interest, some people take it to extremes. Their self-serving behavior ends up causing difficulties for other people in the workplace. Self-serving people come in many forms, but this book focuses on two common types – arrogant people and busybodies.

Dealing with manipulative people and difficult situations requires rational, not emotional, responses. There are constructive ways to defuse potentially explosive problems and create a positive atmosphere in the workplace.

In this book, you'll gain an overview of manipulative behavior in the workplace and learn some effective strategies for dealing with it. You'll understand the characteristics of the various types of manipulative people commonly encountered in a work environment. And you'll learn skills to confront and deal with these types of manipulative people, and be provided with opportunities to practice these skills.

Arrogant people

Arrogant people act as if they are better than everyone else. Based on a fundamental insecurity, their behavior tends toward diminishing others in an effort to make themselves feel more important.

Busybodies

Busybodies are the office gossips, and just about every office has at least one. Busybodies not only engage in gossip, they actively seek out information to pass on to others. In doing so, they hope to enhance their image.

To reduce the effects of self-serving people on your work life, you should begin by trying to understand them better. You need to learn what motivates them and recognize the characteristics of each type of behavior, so that you can then apply appropriate techniques.

In this book, you'll learn about arrogant people and how to deal with them. You'll learn why they act as they do and which actions constitute arrogant behavior. You'll learn to distinguish arrogance from confidence and how to apply a simple three-step, open-close method to deal with arrogant behavior.

You'll also learn about busybodies, what makes them do what they do, why they must be dealt with, and how to use a straightforward strategy for dealing with gossip in the workplace.

After learning how to recognize and cope with these two common types of self-serving people, you will get the opportunity to practice both sets of skills in a realistic scenario. With the knowledge you acquire, you'll be well prepared to defend against the effects of self-serving behavior.

Johan is typically a confident, capable employee. However, his coworker, Alan, has been looking over his shoulder constantly, questioning everything he does and offering endless advice. Johan is trying to take it in stride, but he's beginning to doubt his abilities and resent Alan.

Alan's behavior is typical of a micromanager. "Micromanager" is a term used to describe individuals who assert control by involving themselves in the details – no matter how minute – of their work and the work of others. You can expect certain behavior from micromanaging coworkers.

Need control

Key to the micromanager's behavior is the need to be in control, which stems from a general distrust and lack of confidence in the abilities of others. Micromanagers' need to be in control compels them to constantly seek updates and give input about the work others are responsible for.

Essentially, fear of losing control prevents micromanagers from successfully sharing responsibility for work tasks.

Negatively impact productivity

Micromanagers meddle so much that it negatively impacts overall productivity. They involve themselves in so many things that they slow down the progression of work tasks.

Micromanagers often suffer from having a poor self-image, don't trust others, and need to be needed. They often tend to be anxious, suspicious, and inefficient. Working with micromanagers can be annoying. It's almost certainly frustrating and time-consuming, and typically results in a loss of productivity. It's important to learn how to effectively deal with micromanagers in order to minimize the negative impact on productivity.

Changing the micromanager's behavior is unlikely, so you're better off learning how to deal with this person. Adjusting your expectations and your approach to the micromanaging coworker can help you minimize the negative impact of the micromanaging behavior.

This book provides information on how to recognize micromanagers so you can learn to deal with their behavior, become more productive, and regain independence at work. There are several indicators that will help you identify micromanagers. Once you know you're dealing with a micromanager, the consistent use of a four-step process can help you handle that person appropriately.

Upon completion of this book, you should be more comfortable dealing with micromanaging coworkers when the need arises.

CHAPTER 1. IDENTIFYING DIFFICULT PEOPLE

CHAPTER 1. Identifying Difficult People
SECTION 1 - Common Types of Difficult People
SECTION 2 - The Motivations of Difficult People

SECTION 1 - COMMON TYPES OF DIFFICULT PEOPLE

SECTION 1 - Common Types of Difficult People

The types of difficult people encountered in the workplace can be divided into five general types: aggressive, negative, procrastinating, manipulative, and self-serving. If you can identify the types of difficult people you're dealing with, you can better understand how to deal with their behavior and the issues they bring with them.

BENEFIT OF RECOGNIZING DIFFICULT PEOPLE

Benefit of recognizing difficult people

Difficult people are everywhere. Can you think of a difficult person you've encountered in the workplace? Perhaps a coworker who complains constantly? Or somebody who's never able to meet a deadline?

Difficult people cause all kinds of problems in the workplace and make life miserable for their coworkers. For example, a person who misses deadlines can cause coworkers who are forced to pick up the slack to become resentful. A person who constantly complains can lower morale in the workplace. Being able to deal with a difficult person is a skill that can serve you well in the workplace and can help you avoid or overcome awkward situations.

If you can identify what types of difficult people you're dealing with, you can better determine what motivates them to behave the way they do. Once you know the motivation for their behavior, you can understand how to deal with and or avoid the issues they cause. However, just because you see someone as difficult doesn't mean that person necessarily is.

Your response may have included factors such as gender, race, culture, and religion. All of these can affect behavior in the workplace. It's important to understand these differences and consider them before labeling someone as "difficult." What may seem offensive to one person may seem completely normal to a person from a different cultural background.

For example, one person may see no problem with addressing a superior by the person's first name. However, someone from a different cultural background may see this as a sign of disrespect. Have you ever stopped to think that you could be the one being difficult? If you think about it, you can probably think of times when your behavior has caused problems for someone else.

Before you can think about a plan for dealing with someone who you feel is being difficult, you should look at your own behavior to see if it could be something you did that's causing the problem.

It may be a good idea to talk over the situation with someone you trust, such as a coworker, friend, or family member. This person may be able to help you determine whether it's your behavior that needs to change.

For the most part, people themselves aren't really "difficult." However, they do exhibit difficult behaviors. It's these behaviors that cause negative reactions from others. Some examples of the types of behaviors that can cause problems at work include being negative or disruptive, poor attendance, a lack of focus, or an unwillingness to change.

But what can cause people to exhibit difficult behavior? It may be the environment they're living or working in. Or they may be under a lot of pressure and feeling the effects of stress. It's important to examine the person's behavior over a period of time. Does this person act this way all the time, or is this behavior new? If the behavior is out of the ordinary, the person may simply be having a bad day.

Margaret and Rudy have worked together for years. They've always worked well together and gotten along.

Last week, Margaret asked Rudy for advice on a project she was working on. Rudy responded angrily that he had enough on his own plate without having to do her work too. Because they've always bounced ideas off each other in the past, Margaret was surprised by Rudy's reaction.

Although her first reaction was to get angry herself, Margaret decided to talk to Rudy to see if everything was okay. Rudy revealed that he was under an unusual amount of stress because of an ill family member. By dealing with the situation, Margaret ensured things didn't escalate or affect their working relationship. Difficult behavior needs to be dealt with in a timely fashion. If allowed to continue, it can get worse over time. People who feel that their behavior helps them get what they want have little incentive to change.

Question

What benefit is there to being able to identify the different types of difficult people?

Options:

1. You can better understand how to deal with them

2. You can better understand how to change their personalities

3. You can find ways to avoid them

4. You can ignore their behavior

Answer:

Option 1: This is the correct option. If you understand the type of difficult person you are dealing with, it is easier to understand how to deal with that person.

Option 2: This option is incorrect. In most cases, it's the behavior that's difficult, not the person. The focus should be on dealing with the behavior, not on trying to change the person.

Option 3: This option is incorrect. Avoiding someone that you have to work with won't solve the problem and, in most cases, isn't a realistic solution.

Option 4: This option is incorrect. Ignoring difficult people will not solve anything. They'll continue to behave in ways that disrupt the workplace.

TYPES OF DIFFICULT PEOPLE

Types of difficult people

Most difficult people that you'll encounter in the workplace can be divided into five general types: aggressive, negative, procrastinator, manipulative, and self-serving.

Each type of difficult person exhibits different behavior that requires a different approach.

Aggressive

Aggressive people tend to be rude and intimidating, trying to control others by behaving like bullies on a playground. They may use tactics such as yelling and threatening to frighten coworkers.

Or, in the case of passive-aggressive people, they may try to control you by dropping hints to make you feel sorry for them, rather than just asking you directly for help. For example, they may say something like, "I hope I can finish this project tonight. I'm not feeling well and I may not be in tomorrow," rather than just asking if you could help them finish the project.

Working with Difficult People

In a worst-case scenario, aggressive behavior in the workplace can lead to violence. Consider the example of Megan, a call center supervisor who's in charge of a small group of agents. She holds team meetings once a week to discuss any issues with her agents. During these meetings, she brings up any mistakes she sees being made by agents. She makes sure to use the names of these employees in front of the whole group, belittling them and calling them names.

Megan feels that if she embarrasses these employees, they won't make the same mistake again. That may be, but Megan's group has the highest absenteeism and turnover rates in the call center.

Negative

Negative people complain about everything but never have suggestions for how to improve anything. They only seem to be happy when they're spreading misery to everyone else. Negative people keep their coworkers from getting their work done by constantly distracting them. They also bring the people around them down.

Coworkers may start to ignore negative people, which can lead to another problem. On the rare occasion that the negative people really do have something that needs to be brought to their coworkers' attention, chances are nobody will be listening.

For example, Tyson spends his coffee and lunch breaks complaining to his coworkers about pretty much everything. His boss doesn't understand how hard he works. He doesn't make enough money. He gets passed over for every promotion. Even the weather never seems to suit him. If anybody tries to steer the conversation in another direction, Tyson interrupts to bring the topic back to him and his problems. Whatever anybody else is talking about, he finds a way to see something negative about it.

Tyson's coworkers will do just about anything to avoid him. When he walks into the break room, everyone else suddenly decides it's time to get back to work. But they can't get away that easily. Tyson follows his coworkers back to their desks to complain some more, distracting them from their work.

Procrastinator

Procrastinators find reasons to put off doing their tasks. They often have trouble getting started and spend time thinking of excuses for why they can't get their work done. Procrastinators are often afraid of failure. In their minds, missing a deadline is better than submitting poorly done work. Procrastinators will often have trouble meeting deadlines and require more time to complete a task than their coworkers.

In cases where production depends on a number of tasks being completed by different people, a procrastinator can throw everything off. Coworkers may be forced to pick up the slack and will eventually become resentful.

For example, Joel knows his manager is waiting for a report that she asked him to prepare last week. He knows he needs to get it done soon, as she'll be looking for it. The truth is, Joel hasn't even started the report yet. He's not sure what he needs to do, and he doesn't want to ask his manager because he doesn't want to admit he hasn't started.

Joel decides he'd better get started. But then one of his coworkers asks if Joel has time to help out with something.

Joel decides he should help his coworker first, and then he can get started on the report.

After helping his coworker, Joel is ready to start the report. Then he remembers something else he should do. By the end of the day, he still hasn't started the report. "That's okay" he thinks. "I'll get it done tomorrow." The next day, Joel's manager asks about the report. He tells her that it's almost done, and that he just needs a few more days.

Manipulative

Manipulative people use their charms to coax and maneuver their coworkers to suit their own needs. Manipulators are self-centered and don't care about anyone else's wants or needs. They enjoy being the center of attention – it doesn't matter to them how they get there.

When manipulators run into people who don't give them the answers they want, they often turn to threats to get their way. For example, a manipulator who feels secure in the workplace may threaten to quit if the boss won't give her what she wants. Manipulators see no problem with using whatever tactics they deem necessary to get their coworkers to help them out. However, they would seldom put themselves out to help someone else.

For example, Omar works for a construction company. When he's given a task that he doesn't want to do, he usually convinces one of his coworkers to do it for him instead. His boss asks him to work on the roof of the building, but Omar would rather stay on the ground and interact with people walking by. Omar asks his boss to get someone else to do the work on the roof. He says he hurt his leg and doesn't feel comfortable climbing the ladder to get to the roof.

Omar makes a big deal about it in front of his coworkers. He declares he is more than capable of doing his job on the ground floor. Omar says that it's unfair of his boss to refuse to accommodate him. His boss, who doesn't want to look like the bad guy, asks another worker to take Omar's place on the roof. Omar is pleased with himself. The next time a situation arises, Omar will have another excuse ready to get his way.

Self-serving

Self-serving people believe in getting something for nothing. They don't see value in achieving things through hard work. They tend to believe that what they feel is best for them is really the fair and moral choice. At Maureen's workplace, there's a group that organizes weekly luncheons, with all proceeds going to charity. Every week, Maureen has an excuse for not going. She forgot her wallet or her mortgage payment is due that week and she can't afford to be spending any extra money.

A few times a year, the same group has a free luncheon to thank everyone for all their contributions. Maureen always attends the free luncheons and sees nothing wrong with it. Sometimes, you might think people are being difficult when they really aren't. Saying or doing something you don't like doesn't necessarily make a person difficult.

For example, a boss may need to give corrective feedback to an employee. The employee might be upset about the feedback, but the boss isn't being difficult. She's just doing her job.

Question 1 of 2
Question
Which scenarios show people behaving aggressively?

Working with Difficult People

Options:

1. Your coworker likes to listen to the radio at her desk. You ask her politely to turn down the volume or use headphones, as the noise is distracting. She screams, "If it's such a big problem, why hasn't anyone else complained?"

2. Your coworker is late and asks you to cover for him with the boss. You tell him that you're not comfortable lying. He tells you not to tell the boss if you know what's good for you.

3. Your coworker asks you to switch vacation dates with him, saying those dates are the only time his entire family can get together. You tell him you have plans you can't change and feel resentful that he asked.

4. Your coworker needs to complete a yearly audit of the company's expenses by the weekend. She hates this part of her job and leaves it to the last minute every year. She decides that before she can get started, she needs to organize her workspace.

Answer:

Option 1: This option is correct. By screaming at you, your coworker is trying to intimidate you and force you to back off.

Option 2: This option is correct. By using threats to get his own way, the coworker is exhibiting aggressive behavior.

Option 3: This option is incorrect. The coworker is not being aggressive. He is simply asking if you would be willing to switch vacation dates. The fact that you feel resentful speaks more about your behavior than his.

Option 4: This option is incorrect. The coworker is procrastinating.

Question 2 of 2

Match the scenarios of people displaying difficult behavior to the category of behavior they're displaying.

Options:

A. The boss asks Dana's opinion on a new procedure. Dana says it won't work, but won't suggest ways to improve it.

B. Jason is facing a deadline and is finding the job difficult. He decides to take a break to think about it and work harder the next day.

C. Kate begs her boss for Friday off. The boss explains he is short-handed. She says she'll quit and leave him short-handed every day.

D. Employees can leave early when it's slow, but are expected to stay late when it's busy. Jack always leaves early but never stays late.

Targets:

1. Negative
2. Procrastinator
3. Manipulative
4. Self-serving

Answer:

Dana is being negative. Negative people complain about something but seldom have a suggestion for how to improve it.

Jason is procrastinating. Procrastinators will put things off, telling themselves that they can always finish their tasks later.

The employee is being manipulative. Manipulative people try to coax people into giving them what they want. When they're told no, they'll often resort to threats or insults.

Jack is being self-serving. Self-serving people want everything for themselves, but never want to put themselves out to help anyone else.

SECTION 2 - THE MOTIVATIONS OF DIFFICULT PEOPLE

SECTION 2 - The Motivations of Difficult People

By learning to identify causes and motivations for difficult behavior, you can more easily develop a strategy to effectively deal with the behavior. Difficult behavior can be caused by many things, such as coming from a dysfunctional family, being stuck in the past, or having low self-esteem.

Common motivations for difficult behavior include the desire to get the job done quickly, the desire to get the job done right, the need to get along and belong, and the need for approval.

CAUSES OF DIFFICULT BEHAVIOR

Causes of difficult behavior
When a person acts disruptively in the workplace, coworkers are often quick to label that person as difficult.

In most cases, it's not people that are difficult, but rather their behavior. But why would someone choose to behave in a difficult way? People will often use difficult behavior if, in the past, it's helped them get what they want or need. It's easier to understand difficult people if you can identify the reasons behind their behavior.

The difficult people in your office probably don't see themselves as difficult. In fact, they probably think you're the difficult one. After all, you're what's standing between them and what they want. But if you change your reaction to reflect their behavior types, they may start to think of you as being more reasonable, and in turn, change their reactions and behavior. Realizing that changing your behavior can help to change theirs can help you more easily combat difficult behavior.

In order to deal with a person's difficult behavior, it helps to understand what the person wants and needs.

However, identifying someone's wants and needs may not always be possible. Identifying intent, or what the person hopes to accomplish with his behavior, can be easier. If you have a difficult relationship with a coworker, it may be helpful to ask the person's opinion about why the relationship is difficult. Doing this helps to create a feeling of being in control.

If you choose this approach, it's important to remember that you may not always like what you hear. You need to be able to really listen without taking it personally. By listening to the words and not just reacting, you may find clues to your coworker's motivations and needs.

Your response may have included the most common reason for difficult behavior - someone's needs are not being met. And it's not just about physical needs, but also psychological needs, such as the need for control, recognition, or respect. If somebody has been rewarded for difficult behavior in the past by having his needs met, he has no incentive to change. For example, if every time a coworker interrupts you, you stop what you're doing to listen, the coworker will probably continue to behave this way.

Dealing with the difficult behavior of others isn't easy, and you shouldn't expect instant results. Changing someone's behavior takes time. Difficult behavior can also be caused by deeper issues. Some of these issues include lack of experience, being stuck in the past, and having low self-esteem. Understanding why difficult people behave the way they do can help you develop a strategy to deal with the issues they cause.

Dysfunctional family

People who grow up with a lack of experience in different social settings may have never learned the basic social skills to enable them to interact appropriately with others. For example, someone who wasn't given any privacy while growing up may become an adult who sees nothing wrong with intruding into everyone else's personal lives. This person doesn't understand or respect other people's need for privacy.

Stuck in the past

People who are stuck in the past may exhibit difficult behavior because they relate to people in the present as though they were a specific person who caused them grief in the past. For instance, someone who was treated abusively or unfairly by a previous boss may feel anger toward a new boss because of their unresolved anger. The person behaves badly toward the new boss because, in that person's eyes, the new boss represents someone from the past who caused him pain.

Low self-esteem

People with low self-esteem will often use difficult behavior, such as being demanding or offensive, to keep others at a distance. They do this to protect their own fragile sense of self. As an example, they may have been teased or bullied as children and have learned to respond to others in the same manner.

UNDERSTANDING MOTIVATION FOR BEHAVIOR

Understanding motivation for behavior

Understanding some of the common causes of difficult behavior is a good starting point. However, understanding what motivates someone to behave in a certain way will equip you to develop a strategy to effectively deal with that person's behavior.

Some common types of difficult behavior you may encounter in the workplace are controlling, perfectionist, approval-seeking, and attention-getting. Each type of behavior has a different motivation and requires a different approach.

Controlling

Megan is a call center supervisor who meets with each of her agents individually every month to discuss performance. Megan's biggest complaint with her agents is that they take too long on each call.

She tells the agents that they need to use whatever means necessary to finish the call as soon as possible and move on to the next one. If Megan notices an agent has been on a call for what she thinks is too long, she'll often stand over him while he's talking, giving him disapproving looks while pointing at her watch.

Megan is motivated to get the job done quickly to keep costs down. This causes her to exhibit controlling behavior. Controlling behavior is also a type of aggressive behavior. What Megan needs to understand is that not all calls can be handled that quickly. If customers don't feel that situations are resolved, they may call back repeatedly until they're satisfied.

Megan's agents may need to explain that sometimes it takes time to get to the root of a customer's problem. Megan needs to understand that by taking a little extra time to resolve issues on the first call, her agents are actually cutting back on the number of callbacks and dissatisfied customers. And this saves the company money in the long run.

Perfectionist

Joel is trying to get his report finished and asks a coworker for help. But for every suggestion his coworker makes, Joel finds something wrong with it. "What if that's not exactly what the boss wants?" he thinks. Joel is more afraid of doing something wrong than he is of angering his boss by missing another deadline.

Joel has started his report a number of times. He gets so far, decides he can do better, and starts over. At this rate, he may never get it done. Joel is motivated by a need to get the job done right, which is causing him to behave like a perfectionist. Perfectionists can often be indecisive and overly critical. This is a type of procrastination.

This type of behavior may be brought on by Joel's need for approval. However, his behavior can really slow down a project. Because he doesn't feel like what he's done is good enough, he's unable to move on to the next step. To counteract this behavior, Joel's boss needs to provide him with lots of support and reassurance. Joel's boss needs to make him understand that being able to get a job done well and on time is more important than spending so much time on every little detail.

Approval-seeking

Cindy, a law firm receptionist, has a problem saying no to her coworkers. One coworker, Neil, is constantly late for work and expects Cindy to cover his phone for him. Cindy has told Neil she can't keep covering for him, but she continues to do it anyway. Another coworker is always asking Cindy to help out with typing and filing. Cindy doesn't have time, but says it's no problem, because she doesn't want to be thought of as difficult. She wants her coworkers to like her.

Cindy is having a hard time keeping up at the office, but doesn't want her coworkers to think less of her. But if Cindy is unable to complete all the work she's taken on, somebody will end up angry with her. Cindy is motivated by the need to get along and belong and is exhibiting approval-seeking behavior. She doesn't want to say no to anyone, and will agree to all requests. This may often result in Cindy not being able to do any of her work effectively. Approval-seeking behavior is a type of negative behavior.

Cindy wants to be thought of as the "nice" person, always agreeable and willing to help out. That's why she hasn't been able to stick to her decision to not cover for her coworker. Cindy needs to understand that it's not always possible to please everybody. And, by trying to do just that, she isn't able to do her job effectively and risks making people angry at her. Cindy's boss may help her by taking on the role of the "bad guy" and telling Cindy's coworkers not to ask her for help with their work.

Attention-getting

Maureen likes to be the center of attention at work. During a staff meeting, after the boss is done explaining a new project, she asks if anyone has any questions. One employee raises his hand and asks a question. Maureen immediately interrupts so she can let everyone know what she thinks the answer is.

Her boss then says that she's right, and Maureen is pleased with herself. Later that day, she drops by her boss's office to discuss another idea for the project. Her boss tells her that he's busy at the moment and asks if it can wait. She comes in anyway, saying it will only take a minute. Her boss begrudgingly puts his work aside for the moment to listen to her.

A few hours later, Maureen is back in her boss's office to discuss some more ideas. Her boss is starting to get annoyed, because she's making it difficult for him to get his own work done.

Maureen is motivated by the need to be appreciated and is displaying attention-getting behavior. This is a type of self-serving behavior. She has no problem interrupting others' work by calling or stopping by their offices constantly. She's often seen as a pest by her boss and coworkers. To help mitigate this difficult behavior, Maureen's boss needs to acknowledge her and let her know she is appreciated. Once Maureen gains the approval she's seeking, the situation should start to improve.

Question

Match each example of difficult behavior to the motivation behind it.

Options:

A. Tyrell needs a cost analysis done for a client by end of day. You say you need to meet with the client first. He insists it must be done today.

B. Denise is working on a presentation for a client. She's changed her mind three times about the best way to start it.

C. Noel asks for everyone's input on a project. He agrees to proceed one way, but when another suggestion is offered, he agrees to it too.

D. Jean stops by your office several times a day to let you know about every little accomplishment.

Targets:

1. To get the job done quickly
2. To get the job done right
3. To get along and belong
4. To be appreciated

Answer:

Tyrell is exhibiting controlling behavior, motivated by his desire to get the job done quickly.

Denise is motivated to get the job done right. However, her indecisiveness can make it difficult to get the job done at all.

Noel is trying to be the "nice" person, hoping to get along with everyone. Jean is resorting to attention-seeking behavior in order to feel appreciated.

CHAPTER 2. HOW TO WORK WITH AGGRESSIVE PEOPLE

CHAPTER 2. How to Work with Aggressive People
  SECTION 1 - Dealing with Hostile-aggressive People
  SECTION 2 - Dealing with Passive-aggressive People
  SECTION 3 - Working with Hostile-aggressives

SECTION 1 - DEALING WITH HOSTILE-AGGRESSIVE PEOPLE

SECTION 1 - Dealing with Hostile-aggressive People

Hostile-aggressive behavior has a negative impact on the work environment. It can't be eliminated, but learning to effectively deal with hostile-aggressive people can minimize the negative impact of their behavior.

Working with hostile-aggressive coworkers is one of the most challenging tests of your interpersonal abilities. Hostile-aggressive individuals are bullies and controllers and tend to be pushy, angry, and resentful. They rely on hostile-aggressive behavior to get what they want and don't see anything wrong with their behavior.

You can use a seven-step process to deal with hostile-aggressive behavior. The steps are distancing yourself, assessing the situation, thinking about how you'll respond, assuring the other party you're listening, discussing the problem further, offering your point of view, and monitoring your success.

BENEFITS OF DEALING WITH AGGRESSION

Benefits of dealing with aggression
Does this situation sound familiar to you? Jill and Franco are colleagues. Recently, Franco angrily accused Jill of not pulling her weight. To get Franco off her back, Jill agrees to review a stack of case files that aren't really her responsibility. Jill feels as though she's been bullied into accepting the extra work and her stress level is high.

In this situation, Franco's use of anger to get his way is typical hostile-aggressive behavior. Hostile-aggressives use their bad behavior, such as reacting angrily and being accusatory, to get what they want or to have things their own way.

You will likely face hostile-aggressive behavior at work. You may think ignoring it is a viable option, but this is unrealistic. Also, dealing with hostile-aggressive behavior provides benefits you'll want to take advantage of:

- increased productivity,
- improved self-esteem, and
- a regained sense of control.

Increased productivity

Dealing effectively with hostile-aggressive people helps you reduce the stress caused by their bad behavior. And a less stressful work environment facilitates improved health and increased workplace productivity.

Improved self-esteem

Improved self-esteem is another possible benefit. Suppose you interpret a hostile-aggressive person's behavior as a personal attack – this can be damaging to your self-esteem. Learning to effectively handle hostile-aggressive behavior will reduce its damaging effects, plus you'll feel a sense of accomplishment.

Regained sense of control

It can be hard to deal with hostile-aggressive behavior calmly. You may find yourself losing control or feeling like you've lost control. Knowing how to deal with hostile-aggressive behavior can help you regain your sense of control. This will allow you to avoid being drawn into the negative behavior, so you're part of the solution and not part of the problem.

HOSTILE-AGGRESSIVE BEHAVIOR

Hostile-aggressive behavior
Hostile-aggressive individuals are bullies and controllers. Their general method of operation is to look strong by making others look weak. It's not unusual for them to yell during exchanges with others, and they tend to be offensive, belligerent, and bad listeners. And they typically have a resentful attitude. People with hostile-aggressive personalities are sometimes classified as two types: the verbal assailant and the hothead.

Verbal assailant
Verbal assailants tend to attack with words. They come across as openly abusive and tend to be abrupt, intimidating, and overwhelming. They attack at the personal level and generally pick an aspect of an individual's behavior or personality to fuel the attack.

Hothead
Hotheads are prone to sudden outbursts of anger and rage, even when everything seems to be going well. A hothead's anger tends to be triggered when the individual perceives a physical or psychological threat. The

hothead's anger is likely to be followed by fear and suspicion.

Consider this example of typical hostile-aggressive behavior you might witness when dealing with a verbal assailant. Caroline is a soft-spoken, competent, and knowledgeable woman. She's in a team meeting when she makes a suggestion to build on one of her colleague's ideas. The idea is Candice's, and she has a hostile-aggressive personality.

Follow along to find out how Candice reacts to Caroline's suggestion.

Caroline: What if we add a "worst-case" scenario plan? That way the client will know we're prepared for all possible outcomes.

Caroline says, genuinely.

Candice: What was that Caroline? I couldn't hear you. If you want to be taken seriously, at least have the conviction to express yourself with confidence instead of in a mousy, noncommittal way!

Candice says, angrily.

In this example, Candice felt threatened by Caroline's contribution. True to verbal assailant form, Candice responded with a verbal attack on Caroline. She perceives Caroline's soft-spoken nature as a weakness and angrily attacked Caroline based on this personal characteristic.

Question

Which situations are examples of hostile-aggressive behavior?

Options:

1. Jack ignores Kendra's attempts to contribute during a debate on project work, but angrily shares his negative opinion of her work

2. Ken and Abdul are having a productive discussion when all of a sudden Ken starts yelling at Abdul

3. Shiane retells a personal story to break the ice in a tense project meeting

4. Tito is having a conversation with a customer who becomes belligerent, so Tito calmly informs the customer that he'll terminate the call if she doesn't stop yelling

Answer:

Option 1: This option is correct. Jack's behavior – angry and ignoring Kendra – is classic behavior of a verbal assailant.

Option 2: This option is correct. Ken is a hothead. Hotheads are known to explode into anger from a calm state.

Option 3: This option is incorrect. Retelling an appropriate personal story is a great way to break tension. Shiane isn't demonstrating hostile-aggressive behavior.

Option 4: This option is incorrect. Tito has remained calm in spite of his customer's hostile behavior.

HANDLING HOSTILE-AGGRESSIVE BEHAVIOR

Handling hostile-aggressive behavior
Understanding why a person acts in a hostile-aggressive manner can help you effectively handle this behavior. Where does hostile-aggressive behavior come from? It's a learned behavior. Hostile-aggressive behavior is a form of control. Individuals who interact in a hostile-aggressive way have learned that by being difficult, they get what they want.

Even though they come across as strong and confident, often the reality is that they're frightened and insecure. Acting with hostility and aggression is how these individuals achieve a feeling of safety, power, and control. Have you ever been left feeling bullied or taken advantage of after a dealing with a coworker? If so, you may have been on the receiving end of hostile-aggressive behavior. You may also have been left feeling vulnerable, provoked, angry, frustrated, powerless, or confused.

Question

Working with Difficult People

Suppose you're working on a project with a coworker. You've made a suggestion that you think will improve the project output, but your coworker won't even consider it. In fact, he's being difficult and becoming angry. You just want to give up on your suggestion to end the grief.

How would you handle this behavior?

Options:

1. Work to defuse the person's anger and move toward a solution

2. Attempt to reason with the person and handle the situation with kindness

3. Advise the person that his behavior is unacceptable and refuse to work with him

Answer:

Option 1: This option is correct. Because hostile-aggressives don't see anything wrong with their behavior, the best approach is to work to defuse the person's anger and move toward a solution.

Option 2: This option is incorrect. Reasoning won't work because hostile-aggressives see nothing wrong with their behavior. And kindness is understood by hostile-aggressives as weakness and will therefore just encourage their behavior.

Option 3: This option is incorrect. While the person's behavior is unacceptable, you won't be able to change it and refusing to work with him will likely just anger him even further.

There's a seven-step process that can help you handle hostile-aggressive behavior. The process involves distancing yourself, assessing the situation, thinking about how you'll respond, assuring the other party you're listening, discussing the problem further, offering your point of view, and monitoring your success.

The first step in handling hostile-aggressive behavior is to distance yourself from the situation emotionally, and physically if necessary. Distance yourself by depersonalizing the situation. Remember that the person is probably reacting to an issue or a culmination of issues that actually have nothing to do with you, so it's best that you don't take it personally. It also helps to stay neutral and remain calm.

Taking it personally and failing to stay calm increases the likelihood that you'll react angrily, which will only escalate the situation. It's important that, even though the attack is personal and inappropriate, you don't respond in kind. The second step is assessing the situation. Actively listen while the hostile-aggressive person says all they have to say.

Don't interrupt and don't respond until you have both calmed down. Interjecting while either of you is upset can make things worse. Also, if you're reacting, you're not listening. You may misunderstand and prolong the incident. The third step is thinking about how you'll respond. This helps ensure you respond in the most effective way. When the person is done venting and you can respond, you will move on to step four – assuring the other party you're listening.

Think about how you'll respond

Consider what you've learned from actively listening and think carefully about how you'll respond to effectively address the situation. Remember to hold your commentary until the hostile- aggressive person has finished.

Assure the other party you're listening

Once the person has finished venting, give assurance that you're listening by summarizing what you've understood the person to say.

Now that you have achieved understanding, politely offer to discuss the problem further; this is step five. Such a discussion can improve understanding of the situation, allowing for a speedier and more complete resolution. It can also give you more insight on how to handle the hostile-aggressive person in the future.

In step six, offering your point of view, you can explain how you feel. You should also give the other person an opportunity to reflect, gather thoughts, and return to the discussion if necessary.

The final step, step seven, is to monitor your success. Following a hostile-aggressive encounter, you should take the time to evaluate how well your approach worked. Learn from your successes as well as your mistakes and use this information in future dealings with hostile-aggressive coworkers.

Danica and Jasper are technical writers. They often discuss particular challenges they're facing. Today, Danica is having trouble describing something and has asked Jasper for his input. The discussion is progressing nicely when Jasper comments that he can't believe Danica is having such trouble. Danica immediately and angrily retorts "Well, obviously you can't do any better or you'd be helping instead of criticizing. I don't know why I even bothered to ask!"

Jasper realizes he's made Danica angry and he needs to deal with the situation. He follows several steps:

- he distances himself from the situation by reminding himself that he shouldn't take Danica's outburst personally,
- with his composure intact, he listens carefully to what Danica is saying, and
- he thinks about how he'll respond when she's finished.

Now that Danica has finished, follow along as Jasper attempts to deal with her hostile-aggressive outburst.

Jasper: Danica, I understand what I said was disrespectful. And I understand why you're upset.

Jasper says, sincerely.

Danica: Well I should hope so! Danica says, excitedly.

Danica says, excitedly.

Jasper: I'm willing to explore this situation with you if you'd like. I don't want there to be any bad blood between us.

Jasper says, sincerely.

Danica: No, thanks. I don't see the point of discussing it any further. You understand why I was upset and I appreciate you acknowledging you were wrong.

Danica says, flatly.

Jasper: That's fair, but I would like to point out that I never meant to come across as disrespectful. I was thinking that perhaps you were off your game, under the weather, or stressed, because you usually excel at describing these complex ideas. Can you see that?

Jasper says, kindly.

Danica: Really? Hmm...I guess I can accept that that's where you were going with your comment.

Danica sounds interested.

Jasper: I can see how you could take it wrong. I didn't do a good job of expressing myself. It's important to talk these things through – I don't want a misunderstanding to diminish our work relationship.

Jasper says, kindly.

After his confrontation with Danica, Jasper reflects on the incident. He knew Danica could behave in a hostile-aggressive manner, but had never been on the receiving end before. Now that he has, he knows that a humble approach can help get Danica past her anger and move the situation toward resolution.

Question

Travis and Claudio work at the same company and have similar jobs and responsibilities. This means they work together often. Based on the details of the incident, which aspects of dealing with hostile-aggressive behavior did

Travis perform appropriately?

Options:

1. Distance yourself
2. Assess the situation
3. Think about how you'll respond
4. Assure the other party you're listening
5. Discuss the problem further
6. Offer your point of view
7. Monitor your success

Answer:

Option 1: This option is correct. Travis distanced himself from the situation by not taking Claudio's anger personally. If Travis had taken Claudio's anger personally, he would have risked losing his temper. If he had reacted poorly himself, he might have made the situation worse.

Option 2: This option is correct. If Claudio was still upset, Travis should've keep quiet and assessed the situation without contributing. Anything he said might have fueled Claudio's anger and drawn Travis into a nonproductive, heated exchange instead of just letting Claudio burn out.

Option 3: This option is incorrect. Travis should have listened carefully and thought about how best to respond to help resolve the situation.

Option 4: This option is correct. An effective resolution can only be achieved when mutual understanding exists. Summarizing, in his own words, what Claudio said was a good way for Travis to do this.

Option 5: This option is incorrect. Travis should've offered to discuss the situation with Claudio. This would have opened the door to resolution. Claudio may even have learned that he doesn't need to resort to hostile-aggressive behavior.

Option 6: This option is correct. It's important that Claudio understand that he can talk through problems and get what he wants by asking. Offering to reflect on the situation at a later date opened the door to Claudio's personal growth.

Option 7: This option is correct. It's important that Travis use this as a learning experience. Whatever he's learned he can later apply to situations with Claudio or other hostile-aggressive coworkers.

SECTION 2 - DEALING WITH PASSIVE-AGGRESSIVE PEOPLE

SECTION 2 - Dealing with Passive-aggressive People

Passive-aggressive behavior is difficult to handle because it's subtle. Passive-aggressive individuals seem pleasant and helpful, but are often angry and fearful. They also can't say "no," which means they say "yes" when they really don't want to. This creates resentment in passive-aggressive people. To cope and regain a sense of power and control, they purposely inhibit productive, efficient work.

To build a more positive relationship with passive-aggressive types, follow these steps: start documentation, confront the individual on specific incidents, and provide positive reinforcement. If you try this, and are unsuccessful in getting the passive-aggressive person's cooperation you can try using whatever leverage you have and getting support from your coworkers or supervisor.

PASSIVE-AGGRESSIVE BEHAVIOR

Passive-aggressive behavior
Have you ever had a coworker who seemed pleasant and competent but then let you down? Maybe he agreed to provide data for a project but failed to produce it? Or maybe she agreed to contribute to a project, but didn't?

These are examples of typical passive-aggressive behavior. If you've experienced something like this, maybe you were concerned that you were overreacting or misinterpreting the situation.

Feeling angry is normal when you're on the receiving end of passive-aggressive behavior because anger and fear are the driving emotions behind the behavior. Passive-aggressive behavior is far more subtle than hostile-aggressive behavior and just as hard, if not harder, to handle.

People with passive-aggressive personalities typically come across as quiet and shy. Additionally, you'll notice they're always nice, never defend themselves, and don't assert themselves.

You can also recognize passive-aggressive people by other common behaviors:
- talking about others, in a harmful way, behind their backs,
- playing dumb to either frustrate others or gain some type of advantage,
- not taking responsibility for their actions, and
- rarely saying what they really mean.

Question

What statements accurately describe the behavior of passive-aggressive individuals?

Options:

1. They're quiet and shy on the outside, but angry and fearful on the inside
2. They don't take responsibility for their own actions
3. They fail to keep commitments
4. They're honest and straightforward
5. They are assertive

Answer:

Option 1: This option is correct. Passive-aggressive individuals often come across as quiet and shy, which is a great camouflage for the anger and fear they harbor.

Option 2: This option is correct. Passive-aggressive individuals are skilled at passing off their responsibilities.

Option 3: This option is correct. Consistent failure to keep commitments is a typical passive-aggressive behavior.

Option 4: This option is incorrect. Passive-aggressive individuals are known for rarely saying what they mean.

Option 5: This option is incorrect. Assertiveness is not a skill possessed by passive-aggressive individuals.

Passive-aggressive personality types want to be understood as nice, agreeable, and helpful, and they work very hard to project this image. The key to the behavior of passive-aggressive people is their inability to be assertive. This means they say "yes" when they want to say "no." They commit to work or tasks they don't want to do.

Passive-aggressive people are full of anger and fear. Unable to say "no," they end up doing things they don't want to and feel resentful about it. They sabotage work efforts and avoid fulfilling commitments they've made, all while maintaining a facade of pleasantness. Experience has taught them that this is how to deal with their unexpressed fear and anger. Passive-aggressive behavior may manifest as missed deadlines, broken promises, poorly done work, the silent treatment, and the use of excuses to justify actions.

Based on their typical behavior, passive-aggressive individuals generally fall into one of three categories: the knowledge warden, the unresponsive aggressor, and the waffler.

Knowledge warden

Passive-aggressive types who refuse to part with information in their control are known as knowledge wardens. A knowledge warden will make excuses that you can't reasonably counter without looking insensitive or unreasonable, and then they'll withhold the information you need to do your job.

Unresponsive aggressor

The unresponsive aggressor appears uninterested in communicating and may fail to respond to questions. Unresponsive aggressors may hesitate when asked a question. As they hesitate, you may move on or make a decision without them. This is a stall tactic that is intended to frustrate or impede efficient, productive work.

Waffler

Another passive-aggressive type, the waffler, hates to make decisions, always wants to be on the winning side, and desperately wants the approval of others. The waffler will do whatever it takes to avoid making a commitment. This is a clever way to impede work or exert control over a situation.

Consider this example. During a team meeting, Ava agrees to supply a return on investment (ROI) projection for a project. The ROI results are a major decision-making factor and therefore it's vital that the team have them before moving ahead with the project. Ava secretly resents having been asked to do the ROI. Follow along to find out how Ava reacts as she depicts each of the three passive-aggressive types, and the impact her reaction might have on the project and project leader, Jack.

Knowledge warden: Jack's having a hard time getting the ROI information from Ava. He's tried contacting her via e-mail and phone, but his requests for updates have been ignored. Every time the team has a meeting, Ava pleasantly offers some excuse and insists she's just about done. Meanwhile, the project has stalled. Jack may have to reassign the task.

Unresponsive aggressor: Jack and Ava are meeting to discuss the ROI results. Jack finds getting the information difficult. He's not sure if Ava's silence and hesitation are a sign that the ROI is bad, that there's something wrong with her, or that she's angry with him for some reason. Whatever it is, it's frustrating and a waste of time. He can't spend all day trying to figure out what's wrong – he just needs to know the ROI results.

Waffler: Jack and Ava are meeting to discuss the ROI results. Jack asks questions, but Ava never gives him a straight answer. Ava's the one with the experience, but she insists that Jack decide how to interpret the results. Jack wasn't intending to do any work on this. He expected a completed ROI that the team could use to make a decision. This is slowing down the team's progress.

These examples demonstrate that while each type of passive-aggressive behavior is different in technique, the result is the same. Situations get complicated and passive-aggressive people are able to assert some control over the situation. This helps them act on their resentment while still maintaining a pleasant and helpful persona.

Question

Sonia and Hani are working on a project. Hani is withholding information he's supposed to provide.

Identify the examples where Hani behaves passive-aggressively.

Options:

1. Hani is procrastinating about compiling some data Sonia needs, and he keeps avoiding her

2. In a meeting with Hani, Sonia is surprised by his silence on matters he's supposed to be the authority on, and ends up drawing her own conclusions

3. Hani and Sonia are having a discussion about what action to take, but every time Sonia asks for his advice, all he offers is ambiguous input

4. Hani and Sonia are discussing ways to proceed with a project and Hani volunteers an approach that he is confident will work

5. Hani explodes in anger and attacks Sonia's capabilities when she asks for his opinion on the approach to take on the project

Answer:

Option 1: This option is correct. Hani is exhibiting behavior attributed to the knowledge warden. He is likely procrastinating because he doesn't want to do the work in the first place.

Option 2: This option is correct. Hani is acting like an unresponsive aggressor. Instead of being up front with Sonia, he uses an unresponsive approach.

Option 3: This option is correct. Hani's behavior reflects that of a waffler. His ambiguous input is a way to refrain from making a decision and ultimately complicates the work to be done.

Option 4: This option is incorrect. As a passive-aggressive personality type, Hani would never volunteer an approach.

Option 5: This option is incorrect. Passive-aggressive types like Hani don't usually get outwardly angry. Instead, they maintain a facade of pleasantness and sabotage work efforts as a form of revenge.

HANDLING PASSIVE-AGGRESSIVE BEHAVIOR

Handling passive-aggressive behavior

Handling passive-aggressive behavior is tricky. In fact, the best way to handle it is to not react at all. Passive-aggressive individuals are trying to get a reaction out of you. If they can upset you, all the better. This is the only way they know how to interact. If you don't react, the passive-aggressive behavior will typically stop – for the time being, anyway. When you don't react as expected, the passive-aggressive individual won't know what to do.

Passive-aggressive individuals are usually unaware of their behavior, which is why you really can't do anything to change it. However, assertiveness training has been shown to be an effective way of encouraging passive-aggressive people to learn better ways of interacting with others. Learning how to say "no" – and knowing that it's OK to do so – gives the passive-aggressive person an alternative to always saying "yes" and then being angry about it.

Working with Difficult People

You can use three steps to help you handle passive-aggressive behavior in the workplace. Begin by starting documentation, then confront the individual about specific incidents, and, finally, provide positive reinforcement. The first step in the process is to start documentation. Document when and what you asked the passive-aggressive individual to do. This way, if things go wrong because of a passive-aggressive person's failure to do the job, you can prove that it wasn't your fault.

Perhaps you have to work with someone you know is passive aggressive. Be proactive and start documentation. For example, send an e-mail clearly outlining what you've asked for and expect. The second step in handling passive-aggressive behavior is to confront the individual about specific incidents. Just state what happened and its impact.

For instance, say something like "You agreed you'd deliver the completed paperwork by the end of the day Monday, and you didn't. This means I can't live up to my commitment." Don't get personal and attack the person's character or personality. Keep your focus on the incident itself.

Greg and Anita are coworkers. Anita's supposed to help Greg by photocopying a proposal he's just finished. He's leery about working with Anita because she's let him down in the past. As Greg suspected, Anita didn't photocopy the proposal. Follow along as Greg speaks to Anita about the incident.

Greg: Anita, do you have a moment? I'd like to talk to you privately.

Greg says, seriously.

Anita: Sure Greg, anything for you.

Anita says, pleasantly.

Greg: Anita, I asked you to have the proposal ready at a specific time. I was counting on you and you let me down. I had to stay late to do the work myself.

Greg says, seriously.

Anita: I'm sorry Greg, I couldn't get to the photocopier because Sally in finance was printing off reports. Honestly, the situation was beyond my control.

Anita says, apologetically.

In this brief conversation, Greg did a great job of sticking to the facts and not making the incident personal. Anita was pleasant but still making excuses, a common passive-aggressive tactic. Confronting the individual offers a chance for passive-aggressive people to see you're on to their tactics, hopefully forcing them to find a more appropriate way to interact.

Step three in handling passive-aggressive behavior is to provide positive reinforcement. Positive reinforcement is given only when passive-aggressive individuals do what was asked and expected of them. When this happens, it's important that you acknowledge the effort. Show appreciation for the work they've done by telling them how helpful they were, and the positive impact it had.

Suppose that in the previous example, Anita did get the proposal ready on time. Greg could provide positive reinforcement by saying something like "I just wanted to let you know I got that proposal submitted on time. You did an excellent job compiling and copying the proposal. I really appreciate the work you put in to make that happen. Thank you."

Greg's positive reinforcement might be just what it takes to build a positive, productive relationship with

Anita. This may help Anita see that she doesn't have to be passive-aggressive.

Everyone likes to be acknowledged and appreciated for the work they do. For passive-aggressive individuals, it's a chance to see that contributing can bring positive rewards, and it shows them a different way to interact. The payoff for you is that you build a relationship where you can rely on this individual to do what you ask, allowing you to do your own job more efficiently and productively.

However, if you've tried these steps and been unsuccessful in getting the passive-aggressive person's cooperation, you have a few more options you can try. Select each option to learn more.

Use leverage

If you have leverage, use it. Here, your documentation will be useful. Reminding the passive- aggressive individual of the commitment she made can prompt her to do the work. You can also try reminding her that one day, she may need your help.

Get support from your coworkers

Your coworkers are likely to have knowledge that can help you deal with the passive-aggressive individual, so get support from them. There's also power in numbers. If you and your coworkers

unite, you may be able to convince your supervisor that the negative impact of the passive- aggressive individual's behavior is significant and needs to be dealt with.

Get help from your supervisor

You can also get help from your supervisor. Express how the individual's behavior is negatively impacting your productivity, and ask for advice on how to handle the situation. If you choose to approach your supervisor, make sure you're prepared with facts and specific examples. Again, your documentation will prove useful.

Question

Nadya works with Stanford. She has recently encountered a situation where Stanford let her down. Based on the details of the incident, which aspect of dealing with passive-aggressive behavior did Nadya perform appropriately?

Options:

1. Start documentation
2. Confront Stanford about specific incidents
3. Provide positive reinforcement

Answer:

Option 1: This option is correct. If you know you're working with a passive-aggressive type, it's a good idea to create a paper trail to document your communication about the work to be done. That way if the individual fails to produce the work you need, you can show it wasn't because you weren't clear or reasonable with your expectations.

Option 2: This option is incorrect. If Nadya wants to try and improve her working relationship with Stanford, she can't ignore his behavior. She should confront him and remind him of what he agreed to and tell him that he let her down.

Option 3: This option is incorrect. Stanford is unlikely to change his behavior based on false flattery. Nadya should only give positive reinforcement when it's truly deserved.

SECTION 3 - WORKING WITH HOSTILE-AGGRESSIVES

SECTION 3 - Practice: Working with Hostile-aggressives

Working with hostile-aggressive individuals can be extremely difficult. Above all else, always keep your own anger in check and your attitude professional. Applying a process that involves distancing yourself, assessing the situation, thinking about how you'll respond, assuring the other party you're listening, discussing the problem further, offering your point of view, and monitoring your success can help you handle hostile-aggressive behavior you encounter in your workplace. The more you face hostile-aggressive behavior, the better you'll be at handling it.

WORKING WITH HOSTILE-AGGRESSIVE PEOPLE

Working with hostile-aggressive people

You'll likely face hostile-aggressive behavior at work. Being prepared for it can help you handle the situation more effectively and minimize the impact of the negative behavior. You'll recognize hostile- aggressive individuals by their difficult behavior, which is likely to be laced with hostility, anger, and resentment. Their exchanges often involve yelling and offensive and belligerent behavior.

Effectively handling hostile-aggressive people so you can get back to work takes finesse. A seven-step process can help.

Consider this example. A home renovation company has spent countless hours trying to satisfy a customer who can't be satisfied. George, the operations manager, is not happy. He thinks the company should cut its losses and let the customer go. James, the customer care manager, wants to make things right and turn this experience into a good one for the customer.

Working with Difficult People

George storms into James's office, shaking his fist and yelling. Follow along to find out what George had to say.

George: "What are you thinking? I don't think you are thinking! The customer is not always right, James!"

George: "Mrs. Hutchins is unreasonable and can't be pleased. Our work is impeccable. I can't justify the expense, and while we cater to her, my guys are falling behind schedule with other projects."

George: "The problem is she keeps changing her mind. How long are we going to pay for her indecisiveness? Come on James – get real and dump Mrs. Hutchins."

James is taken aback by George's outburst. His anger is overwhelming, but James remembers the first rule of dealing with hostile-aggressive behavior and emotionally distances himself from the situation. He knows this isn't personal and that George is just frustrated with the situation.

Instead of interrupting, James allows George to speak his mind. Meanwhile, he listens carefully to make sure he picks up on the relevant information. This will help him respond more appropriately when George is finished. James thinks acknowledging George's concerns about the loss and the impact on other projects will be a good way to respond.

Now that George is done venting and has calmed down, James feels he can begin a discussion by recapping George's valid points, leaving his emotions out of it. Follow along as James and George explore the situation and look for mutual ground.

James: George, I understand that we're losing money on this project. And the impact on other projects is something we will have to address immediately. Would you like to discuss how we'll handle this now?

James says, concerned.

George: Well, there's no time like the present. And since we've got our cards on the table, let's get this over with.

George says, abruptly.

James: I'm concerned as well. And I agree that Mrs. Hutchins is difficult to work with. She's taking advantage of our commitment to customer satisfaction by changing her mind about what she wants.

James says, calmly.

George: I'm glad to hear it; I was beginning to wonder if you'd lost your senses.

George says, relieved.

James: I have a proposal. I'll contact Mrs. Hutchins and explain our predicament. We'll finish the work upholding our exemplary standards, but we won't make any further design, material, or aesthetic changes unless she wants to pay. Does that sound fair?

James says, calmly.

George: I have one concern. I can't keep dedicating resources to her job at the expense of other customers. If she's willing to pay for additional changes, we'll do them, but she'll have to wait.

George sounds concerned.

James: I agree. That sounds fair. I'll do my best to make sure she feels the same.

James says, enthusiastically.

At this point, James offers to discuss the matter further if George thinks of any other concerns after he leaves James's office. James also invites George to share anything

Working with Difficult People

he thinks will help resolve the issue with Mrs. Hutchins. At the end of the day, James makes notes about this incident. He hopes that by noting what worked and what didn't he will learn how to effectively work with George.

James used the seven-step process to work with George. Distancing himself emotionally allowed him to remain calm. Listening and not interrupting helped James focus on what George was saying and gave him time to think about how he'd respond. Remaining polite and positive as he discussed the issue helped James build rapport and move toward resolution of the issue. While, offering his input helped further express his interest in George's concern. Finally, monitoring his success will help James learn from the experience.

PRACTICE: WORK WITH HOSTILE-AGGRESSIVES

Practice: work with hostile-aggressives
Question
You're the service manager at a car dealership. As you perform your duties, you sometimes need to work with sales people. You are about to have a run in with one of them.

Which examples demonstrate what you should do while Robert vents?
Options:
1. While surprised and a bit alarmed, you don't take Robert's attack personally

2. You listen carefully as Robert expresses himself, and are careful not to interrupt

3. As Robert continues, you consider the facts you can piece together and prepare a response you think will help resolve the situation

4. You tune out Robert's ranting and start formulating your rebuttal

5. You hope that by listening carefully and not speaking, this incident will blow over with the end of Robert's outburst

Answer:

Option 1: This option is correct. If you take Robert's hostile-aggressive attack personally, you run the risk of escalating the incident by getting upset yourself.

Option 2: This option is correct. Interrupting could upset Robert even more. He won't be ready to hear whatever you have to say.

Option 3: This option is correct. Taking the time to prepare your response makes good sense. Knowing how you'll approach Robert once he's finished venting could help you resolve the situation quicker.

Option 4: This option is incorrect. You can't resolve the issue if you're not listening to find out why Robert's upset.

Option 5: This option is incorrect. It's unrealistic to believe the incident will resolve itself. You need to listen carefully so you can consider how to respond and address the situation.

CHAPTER 3. HOW TO WORK WITH NEGATIVE PEOPLE

CHAPTER 3. How to Work with Negative People
SECTION 1 - Types of Negative People
SECTION 2 - Dealing with Whiners and Complainers
SECTOR 3 - Dealing with Blamers

SECTION 1 - TYPES OF NEGATIVE PEOPLE

SECTION 1 - Types of Negative People

Negative behaviors in the workplace can impact harmfully on coworkers and derail productivity. The benefits of recognizing and effectively dealing with negative behavior in the workplace are increased productivity, a positive outlook, and the prevention of the escalation of negative behavior.

There are three very common types of people that manifest negative behavior. Whiners focus on themselves with the purpose of gaining sympathy and attention. Complainers believe they know what's right and focus on specific people or issues. And blamers shift responsibility for their actions away from themselves by attributing problems to other people or situations.

NEGATIVE BEHAVIOR

Negative behavior
Many people spend more than half their waking lives at work. When you're at work, your efforts are rewarded, you form friendships and alliances, and often, it's where your core identity is formed. And most people treasure their ability to communicate, socialize, and relate to coworkers in an effective and constructive manner.

Human interaction is part of the social fabric of the workplace. So it's not surprising many issues that arise in the work environment are "people" problems. Every workplace has a unique blend of people, most of whom are committed to doing the work necessary to develop positive work relationships.

But coworkers have different temperaments, reactive styles, and methods for interacting with others. When you work with other people, sooner or later, you're going to be confronted with negative behavior. It's important to remember that everyone – even you – can be negative from time to time. But when negative behaviors begin to cause harm to others or derail productivity, it's time to take action.

Negativity can have a detrimental effect on individuals, teams, and organizations.

- One of the consequences of negativity is reduced productivity. When negative behaviors are accepted, they can permeate the workplace and become the norm. Workers in a negative environment spend more time looking for problems than striving to meet their goals.
- Negativity can seriously damage work relationships. Coworkers on the receiving end of negative behaviors can become withdrawn, resentful, or even hostile toward the perpetrator. This can directly affect the cohesion of departments, teams, and workgroups.
- People who manifest negative behavior can affect morale in the workplace. Negativity can be contagious. These perennial "wet blankets" dampen the enthusiasm of coworkers by casting a negative light over their efforts and enthusiasm.

You'll gain clear benefits when you can recognize and effectively deal with negative behavior in the workplace:

- you'll increase productivity,
- you'll protect your positive outlook, and
- you'll prevent negative behavior from escalating.

You'll increase productivity

Difficult people decrease productivity because their negative behavior affects work relationships and team cohesion. Coworkers often react to difficult people by using avoidance. This is particularly problematic when those people are experts in their field or have skills or training necessary to reach team objectives. By learning how to deal with negative people, you can effectively use them as a resource and increase your own productivity.

You'll protect your positive outlook

People who demonstrate negative behavior can emotionally drain coworkers because they cause frustration and stress. Recognizing and dealing effectively with negative behavior can protect your positive outlook and prevent the danger of reacting angrily, obsessing about the situation, or becoming apathetic about your work.

You'll prevent negative behavior from escalating

Negative behavior is communication in the form of manipulation. If you don't recognize and deal with the behavior, you subtly signal that it's OK to behave that way. This can escalate problems by encouraging negative people to push the limits of acceptable behavior.

Difficult people often have specific behavioral traits that make them identifiable and, in some ways, predictable. By recognizing and categorizing negative behavior, you can take steps to deal with it.

Three very common behavior types express negativity in the workplace:
- whiners,
- complainers, and
- blamers.

RECOGNIZING WHINERS

Recognizing whiners

In general, the difference is focus. Whiners are most often focused on themselves and their perceived burdens – the "poor me" syndrome. Complainers usually focus their negativity outwardly on specific people or issues, and they aren't content until they feel the perceived problem is resolved.

The first common type of negative behavior is whining. Whiners are inwardly focused. They want things to be different, but they don't really know how it should happen. They feel unjustly burdened by the collective expectations of bosses and coworkers. But rather than focus on resolving specific problems, whiners search for general affirmation of their status as victims. They want sympathy and attention, rather than solutions.

Whining is one of the least effective forms of protest, yet it's one of the most common forms of expression in the workplace. Most people whine once in a while. Whining can relieve stress or help you blow off a little steam. But continual whining irritates and annoys coworkers. They may ostracize the whiner, or worse, get caught up in competing with the whiner for attention.

You can recognize whiners from the way they express their negativity in the workplace. Whiners use generalized, self-centered words like I, always, never, everyone, me, or nobody. Their message is one of self-pity – life is unfair, nobody listens, they're being treated poorly, and nobody appreciates what they do. They also make use of superlatives, absolutes, and emphasizers – phrases like "the worst," "most awful," "absolutely cannot," or "so bad."

Rosalie works as a creative director at a large advertising and communications company. The nature of her work means she has to deal with many people in different departments. And because much of her work is project based, she depends on keeping positive relationships with coworkers. This is especially important for those people she depends on to help her meet project deadlines.

Rosalie often works with James, a copywriter. James has been known to indulge in whiny behavior. Follow along as Rosalie talks to James about their current project.

Rosalie: Hi, James. How's everything going? Did you get my notes about the new project?

Rosalie smiles

James: Yes, along with all the other correspondence everybody keeps piling on my desk. Nobody seems to care I have a full workload already.

James whines

Rosalie: Is there a specific problem?

James: It's just unfair that everyone expects me to do everything all the time. I'm only one person. I absolutely can't do what seems to be expected of me in one eight-hour day. It's so frustrating.

James says, whining

Rosalie: Well, the new project schedule is pretty important. I hope you'll go over my notes soon.

James: I swear, this is just the worst day ever. Everyone is after me, and I have a headache. The whole world seems to want a piece of James. You know?

Rosalie: Well, I'll check back with you a little later about those project notes.

Neutrally, Rosalie says

James was demonstrating whining behavior. His comments were self-centered, and they were generalized and unfocused on any real solution to his perceived plight. Most tellingly, James demonstrated self-pity in an attempt to gain sympathy and attention from Rosalie.

RECOGNIZING COMPLAINERS

Recognizing complainers

The second common type of negative behavior is complaining. Complainers differ from whiners in that they're most often focused on specific issues or people. Complainers don't like to compromise. They often have a strong sense for how they think things should be, and any deviation from that produces complaints.

Complainers are easy to recognize because of the way they express negativity in the workplace. They're usually the first to gripe about what's wrong and declare why things won't work. They put as much effort into finding fault as they do in dealing with issues. They love the word "but," as in "It's fine, but..."

Complainers often use phrases like "do it my way," "it would be better," "if only," "we've been through this," "I know what's wrong," or "you're wrong."

They may have been rewarded for the behavior in the past and now view themselves as analysts rather than innovators. They may be genuinely trying to help but lack the communication skills to make things happen. Some have a particular image of the way things should be and a high level of frustration with any deviation.

But most often, complainers feel powerless to effect change, so they point out issues in the hope that someone else will take charge of fixing them. Although you may find it tempting to dismiss them, you should always keep in mind that complainers can be valuable at times. People who try to identify potential faults and problems can be an asset when you need critical thinking about ideas or issues.

But chronic complainers can unnerve and demoralize people who have to deal with them. Complainers rarely hold back from pointing out other people's shortcomings. Complaining behavior annoys and alienates coworkers. It can cause them to become defensive and push back with complaints of their own.

Or they may get into the habit of ignoring or avoiding the complainer, meaning any good ideas, talents, or expertise the complainer possesses will be underutilized.

Rosalie is talking to Chantal, an accountant at the advertising and communications company where they both work. Rosalie has worked with Chantal before and knows she has a reputation for indulging in complaining behavior. Follow along as Rosalie discusses expense claims with Chantal.

Chantal: Hi, Rosalie. It's Chantal. I'm calling about the personal expense claims you submitted last week.

Rosalie: Hi, Chantal. I hadn't heard anything and I was wondering what was going on.

Chantal: Well, you could've called me. Anyway, I found something wrong. You didn't fill out the expense forms the way I requested.

Rosalie: Oh, what's the problem?

Rosalie is puzzled

Chantal: Rosalie, we've been over this before, and you should know how I like to work. You should use a more readable font when printing out the document.

Rosalie: So my expenses are delayed because you didn't like the font I used?

Rosalie is slightly annoyed.

Chantal: Yes, but that's not the point. It's not my job to fix things for you. This system runs smoothly as long as employees are careful and do things the way I say they should be done.

Rosalie: Yeah. We wouldn't want to panic the stockholders over a font issue.

Rosalie is slightly annoyed, but trying to lighten things up.

Chantal: Funny. But you still have to redo your expenses. The right way, this time.

Rosalie: Well, next time maybe you could get back to me sooner if there's a problem. Or better yet, send me an e-mail. Use any font you like.

Rosalie became annoyed by Chantal's inflexibility and dictatorial tone. Unfortunately, Rosalie reacted defensively by pushing back with a complaint of her own. She also took a step to avoid dealing directly with Chantal, by requesting the use of e-mail. This complaining-defensive cycle is detrimental to work relationships.

RECOGNIZING BLAMERS

Recognizing blamers
The third common type of negative behavior is blaming. Blamers avoid admitting their own mistakes and shortcomings by shifting the blame to someone or something else. Problems are rarely their fault. If blamers ever admit to having done something wrong, they'll justify it by claiming they were provoked. The blamer's automatic response is to "point the finger." By deflecting focus away from themselves, blamers avoid responsibility, often at the expense of coworkers.

Blamers have the worst qualities of whiners and complainers. They're often critical and judgmental, yet rarely offer any solutions to problems or issues. If you don't deal with whining and complaining, these behaviors can escalate into blaming behavior. Whiners may indulge in blame if they're not getting the attention they seek. And like whiners, blamers often set themselves up as victims.

Complainers may become blamers when they think they're being ignored or their advice isn't followed.

Blamers also think they know where problems lie — anywhere but with themselves.

Why blamers blame

Blaming is sometimes a defense mechanism. Blamers may be trying to cover up incompetence or may be genuinely afraid of responsibility. They use blame to keep attention away from their own weaknesses or inability to resolve issues. Other times blame is offensive — used as a weapon to discredit coworkers or to "get back" at someone who's blamed them in the past.

You can often recognize blamers by their litany of excuses:

- "I couldn't help it"
- "Everyone does it that way"
- "She told me to"
- "Someone else must have taken it"
- "If you wanted it that way, you should have said so," or "It's not my fault"

Rosalie is talking to Vijay, a graphic designer, about his input to an important advertising campaign. Vijay has been known to use blaming behavior. Follow along as Rosalie talks to Vijay about designs for the project.

Rosalie: Vijay, have you got the revised designs for the new advertising campaign? They were supposed to be done today.

Vijay: I don't know anything about any design revisions.

Rosalie: The deadline is tomorrow. We discussed this at the last team meeting.

Vijay: I don't think that happened. Anyway, you should've sent me a memo if it was that important.

Rosalie: It would've been included in the action items on the minutes of the meeting.

Vijay: I don't think I got those minutes. Your assistant probably forgot to include me when he sent the minutes out.

Rosalie: He e-mailed the minutes out last week and I know you're on the list. Vijay: The system must have had a glitch. That's why you should double check with people if you need something from them.

Rosalie: I need those designs by tomorrow, Vijay.

Vijay: You should have asked me earlier. Shelley and Andrew both have stuff they need from me today. If you think your work is more important than theirs, go tell them. You can't expect me to choose sides.

Rosalie: Vijay, we're going to miss the deadline if you don't get those revisions to me.

Vijay: Now Rosalie, this is your problem, not mine. It wouldn't have happened if you were better organized. And if I may say, you're not going to get anywhere by being a bully.

Vijay was demonstrating blaming behavior. Blamers shift responsibility away from themselves and rarely offer any solutions to issues that arise. When Rosalie asked Vijay about the work he was supposed to have done, he blamed Rosalie's assistant, the e-mail system, his coworkers, and Rosalie herself.

MANAGING NEGATIVITY

Managing negativity

Rosalie is dealing with three negative behavior types in her workplace. James is a whiner, Chantal is a complainer, and Vijay is a blamer. But there's hope for Rosalie if she follows three steps for dealing with negative behavior. Step one is listen to the person who's being negative, step two is to demonstrate an understanding of their message, and step three is to try to resolve the issue. This strategy will help Rosalie increase her productivity, protect her positive outlook, and prevent her coworkers' negative behavior from escalating any further.

Question

Match the negative behavior types to the statements that best exemplify that behavior. You may use each behavior type more than once.

Options:
A. Whiner
B. Complainer
C. Blamer

Targets:

Working with Difficult People

1. "You're picking on me."
2. "I always have too much work."
3. "We need to get a new copier now, before that old one breaks down again."
4. "You didn't do that my way. Let me show you."
5. "It's not my fault."
6. "He told me to do it."

Answer:

Whiners focus on themselves and their perceived burdens – the "poor me" syndrome.

Whiners focus on themselves and rarely offer any specific examples or solutions.

Complainers usually focus outwardly on a particular person or issue they perceive to be a problem.

Complainers are usually set on their own solutions to problems and don't like deviation from what they think is right.

Blamers deflect any responsibilities away from themselves and on to other people.

It's typical of blamers to avoid admitting their own mistakes by shifting the blame to someone else.

SECTION 2 - DEALING WITH WHINERS AND COMPLAINERS

SECTION 2 - Dealing with Whiners and Complainers

The strategy for dealing with difficult people at work consists of three basic steps. Step one is listening to the person who's being negative, and step two is demonstrating you understand the message by acknowledging and summarizing the issue.

When you're dealing with whiners and complainers, step three is attempting to resolve the issue by asking a series of gentle probing questions. With whiners, you'll need to get them to focus on specifics, rather than letting them indulge in general lamentation. With complainers, you'll need to get them to focus on solutions, rather than just criticism.

NEGATIVITY IN THE WORKPLACE

Negativity in the workplace

In today's fast-paced, technically focused world, it's easy to forget that a workplace is made up of human beings with real and sometimes unpredictable emotions. Sometimes, these emotions can manifest in the form of negative behaviors such as whining, complaining, and blaming.

Dealing with negative behavior

You'll often just have to put up with difficult people. But it's appropriate and imperative to deal with whiners, complainers, and blamers when their behavior is negatively affecting your work or the productivity of your team.

Your most important resources are the people you work with. So when the negative behavior of difficult coworkers impacts your productivity, you'll have to take action. But what can you do? Difficult people don't change their behavior overnight. They don't change because you've confronted or shunned them, or just because you've told them to.

What makes them change is your positive, consistent, and solution-oriented approach to building and nurturing your work relationships. When you deal with difficult coworkers, it's important to be a role model for how you want them to behave. Don't buy in to their negativity, and don't fall into the trap of competing with them.

You need to take a positive, proactive approach when dealing with difficult coworkers. Reflecting back negativity only escalates problem behavior.

Whining

Don't whine. This just affirms that whining behavior is acceptable. A positive and realistic approach shows whiny coworkers they aren't powerless to change what they don't like.

Complaining

Don't complain, at least not without proposing a solution to the problem. Being proactive shows your boss you have initiative. It also shows your coworkers that when you take ownership of an issue, you're on the road to solving it.

Blaming

Don't blame. Take responsibility for your actions instead of pointing at someone else. If an issue arises that's somebody else's fault, be constructive about how the problem can be resolved and prevented from happening in the future.

STEPS FOR DEALING WITH NEGATIVE PEOPLE

Steps for dealing with negative people

The main purpose of developing a strategy for dealing with negative people is to change the dynamics of their relationships with you. By following this strategy, you can encourage your coworkers to self-regulate their behavior and make working with them easier.

The strategy for dealing with negative people at work consists of three steps:
1. listen to the person who's being negative,
2. demonstrate you understand the message, and
3. try to resolve the issue.

The three steps for dealing with negative people are the same when you're dealing with whiners, blamers, and complainers. But how you implement the third step – trying to resolve the issue – is different when you're dealing with blamers. In this topic, you'll learn about how to use the three steps when you deal with whiners and complainers.

The first step for dealing with a negative person is to simply listen to what's being said. Listening helps you determine what type of negative behavior is being displayed and also whether what this person is saying has any intrinsic value. Keep in mind it's easier to get people on your side if you give them a little of what they're seeking. Whiners are searching for attention; complainers want acknowledgement.

When you listen, it's important for you not to voice any judgment. At this point, it doesn't matter if the issues are true, valid, or relevant. By just listening to your coworker, you'll help create empathy and establish a base for your relationship. After you've listened to your difficult coworker, the second step is to demonstrate an understanding of the issue. You can do this by defining and summarizing the content and emotion of what your colleague has just relayed to you.

Because your goal is to head toward a better relationship, keep it friendly and positive. Speak to your coworker in the type of voice you'd like to listen to. Request affirmation or acknowledgement of your assessment of the issue. This will build trust so you can both move on to the third step.

Question

Do you think it's important to agree with a difficult colleague when you're demonstrating an understanding of their issues?

Options:
1. Yes
2. No

Answer:

Acknowledging that you've understood the message your difficult coworker is communicating doesn't mean you have to agree with what they're saying. At this point, your purpose isn't to pass judgment but to build on the empathy you've established to create a relationship of understanding and trust.

Now that you've listened to your colleague and demonstrated you understood – but not necessarily agreed with – the message, it's time for the third step – resolving the issue. For difficult coworkers, the issue is the problem – or problems – they're reacting to.

For you, it's the negative behaviors these problems stimulate in your coworkers – behaviors that will affect your ability to do your work. It's not up to you to simply take over your colleague's problems. This would only validate the negative behavior. The purpose of this third step is to change your relationship with your coworker by eliminating the negative behavior and replacing it with another, more acceptable, behavior.

WHINERS AND COMPLAINERS

Whiners and complainers
In the first and second steps for dealing with negative people, you establish empathy and build trust with your negative coworkers. Now is the time to validate their right to resolve the issue on their own.

Implementing the third step – resolving the issues that stimulate negative behavior – is different for whiners and complainers than it is for blamers. For both whiners and complainers, you'll need to ask gentle probing questions that refocus their attention on resolving issues. You can tailor these questions based on the information you gather during the listening stage and the demonstrating understanding stage.

Each of your questions should have a purpose. Whiners need to be focused on the specifics of what's causing their negativity. Complainers need to be focused on coming up with solutions, rather than just pointing out problems. You can phrase questions in many different ways to subtly suggest to your negative coworkers that they need to come up with their own problem-solving decisions:

Working with Difficult People

- What specifically is the problem?
- What have you done to deal with the problem?
- Who could you speak to that might help?
- What's bothering you?
- What exactly did he do?
- What will you do about it?
- What's the solution to this issue?

If your coworkers continue to be negative, don't reward them with sympathy or attention. Shift the conversation and questions back to the issues at hand.

Sometimes you might find it difficult or impossible to make any progress changing the dynamics of your relationships. Conflict resolution is often more effective when handled by an authoritative third party. You shouldn't be reluctant to follow proper business channels if your coworker's negative behavior continues. If you find the negative behavior doesn't stop, document your concerns to the appropriate authority. Management will normally respond to this sort of issue quickly when you're clear about the negative impact on productivity.

Rosalie works as a creative director at a large advertising and communications company. She recognizes that James, a copywriter, indulges in whiny behavior. Follow along as Rosalie goes through the three steps of dealing with negative people.

Rosalie: Hi, James. I'm checking back to find out how you've progressed with reading the project notes I left with you. I need your input so I can submit the report at the end of the week.

James: What a day this has been. My phone has been ringing off the hook. About those notes, I haven't gotten around to them yet.

Rosalie: Tell me what the problem is.

James: Problem? Oh, well I'm just really, really busy.

Rosalie: I'm listening.

James: Well, I've got several projects on the go right now. You know how it is. I'm working so hard I'm going to make myself ill.

Rosalie: Just so I understand, what you're saying is that you haven't read my notes because you feel you've been too busy with other projects. Am I understanding that correctly?

James: I guess so.

Rosalie: Which of the other projects have deadlines that are coming up this week?

James: Well, umm. None this week. But I'm really stressed right now, and I have a dentist appointment I have to get to.

Rosalie: Since our deadline needs to be met, what will help you get to reading the project notes today?

James: Well, I could ask Reception to hold my calls for an hour. But those people never listen to me.

Rosalie: Thanks, James. I appreciate the effort. I'll go with you and we'll get Reception to hold your calls while you read the project notes. I'll touch base tomorrow morning and get your input for my report. How's that for a plan?

James: It sounds doable.

Rosalie followed the three steps for dealing with negative people when she spoke to James. First, she listened to what he had to say to create some empathy in the relationship. Second, she demonstrated she understood his message by summarizing the issue. Third, she asked James a series of gentle probing questions to steer him away from the whining behavior and specify what could be done to resolve the issue. And Rosalie did a great job of not getting drawn back in when James attempted to revert back to his whiny behavior.

Case Study: Question 1 of 2

Scenario

Saul is an accounts manager at a large executive recruitment agency. In the course of his work, Saul often deals with Gail, a manager in the Human Resources Department.

Question:

Which of the three steps for dealing with negative people did Saul apply correctly when he dealt with Gail's whining behavior?

Options:

1. Listen to the person who's being negative
2. Demonstrate understanding
3. Try to resolve the issue

Answer:

Option 1: This option is correct. Saul correctly performed the first step. By listening to Gail, Saul establishes an empathetic bond with her.

Option 2: This option is correct. By defining and summarizing what Gail is saying, Saul correctly performed the second step. He's steering her toward defining and acknowledging the specifics of the issue.

Option 3: This option is incorrect. Saul didn't perform the third step, which was to validate Gail's right to resolve the issue. In this case, he hasn't secured any commitment from Gail that she'll follow through with providing him the information he needs.

Case Study: Question 2 of 2

How should Saul have correctly implemented the third step of his strategy for dealing with difficult people?

Options:

1. Saul should have offered to compile the list of recent hires himself, to alleviate Gail's workload

2. Saul should have asked Gail gentle probing questions to gain her commitment to resolving the issue

3. Saul should have just kept listening to Gail's complaints

Answer:

Option 1: This option is incorrect. Saul won't resolve the issue by doing Gail's work for her. In the third step, he needs to secure her commitment to a positive resolution of the issue.

Option 2: This is the correct option. In the final step, Saul should have asked Gail a series of questions that subtly suggest she commit to her own problem-solving decisions.

Option 3: This option is incorrect. Saul listened during the first step of the strategy. During the third step, Saul should have asked Gail questions based on the information he gathered in the listening stage and the demonstrating understanding stage.

By following the three steps for dealing with negative people, you'll impart a valuable message to your coworkers – negative behavior won't get them what they want. And you'll all benefit from positive and productive working relationships.

SECTOR 3 - DEALING WITH BLAMERS

SECTOR 3 - Dealing with Blamers

To deal with negative people, you follow three steps: listen to the person who's being negative, demonstrate you understand the message, and try to resolve the issue.

When dealing with blamers, you have two options for implementing step three – resolving the issue. When you're at fault, you should own up to your responsibility, acknowledge what the blamer is saying, and ask what you can do to help resolve the issue. When the blamer is at fault, you should confront that person with specific examples of the problem and then work together to resolve the issue.

BLAMERS

Blamers
Everyone makes mistakes. In fact, human error can occur in an almost infinite number of ways. But at work, individuals who are experienced and knowledgeable are expected to anticipate negative outcomes and avoid them. When workplace errors inevitably occur, employees have two choices: accept responsibility or play the "blame game."

Blamers share a common characteristic – they find it easier to attack a person or situation than to tackle a problem. But there isn't just one type of person who becomes a blamer. A number of different causes can cause blaming behavior. Some people consider it a sign of weakness to accept responsibility, or they view any criticism as a personal attack. Other people may be frightened to face what they've done because in the past they've suffered punishment for making mistakes.

Blamers may be protecting their egos or reputations. They may be bullies or the type of person who just can't admit they're wrong. At worst, they may be sly manipulators looking for opportunities to benefit at the expense of others.

The three steps for dealing with negative people are the same for blamers as they are for other negative behaviors like whining and complaining:
1. listen to the person who's being negative,
2. demonstrate you understand the message, and
3. try to resolve the issue.

The difference between dealing with whiners and complainers and dealing with blamers is in how you implement step three – resolving the issue. Dealing with blamers is an essential workplace skill. When you work with other people, it's inevitable that someday you'll be blamed for something. It may be something simple – you forgot to send a reminder about a meeting – or something major that can affect your career – your actions lost a client or caused an accident. And sometimes the blamers will be absolutely right.

How you resolve issues with blamers depends on whether the responsibility for the issue lies with you or with them.

When you're at fault

When you're at fault, owning up to your responsibility is best. Acknowledge what the blamer is saying, and ask what you can do to help. Once you take ownership of the issue, you can apologize, clarify what happened and why, seek a solution, and move on. It's important to make clear that you're more interested in resolving the issue than in being right.

When they're at fault

When blamers are at fault, you'll need to confront them. Blamers will usually stop their negative behavior when you give them specific examples of how their mistakes, miscalculations, or omissions caused the issue. Don't be vague. Blamers find it difficult to shift the blame when you're precise.

Remember that blamers associate responsibility with negative consequences. They won't respond to an attack. Be nonthreatening and diplomatic when you present your position. This will help blamers feel like it's safe to accept responsibility if they're wrong and will give them ownership in the solution if they're right. It also helps to create empathy. For example, you might tell them about a time when you made a mistake, accepted responsibility, and moved on.

Using gentle, probing questions can help you steer blamers away from negative blaming behavior and toward positive problem solving. Keep your questions simple at first and make use of closed-ended questions. Don't give blamers the chance to reinterpret facts to create the impression that they were right all along – either in what they did or in blaming you.

Rosalie is in the staff room of the advertising and communications company where she works as a creative director. She's just encountered her coworker, Vijay, who's upset with Rosalie because she's missed a meeting. Follow along as Rosalie deals with Vijay's blaming behavior.

Vijay: Rosalie, where were you this morning?

Vijay is annoyed.

Rosalie: This morning? I'm not sure I understand. Just tell me exactly what the problem is and I'll listen.

Rosalie is confused.

Working with Difficult People

Vijay: I just got out of our 11:00 meeting with the clients. You were supposed to be there to help me with the presentation, but you didn't show up.
Vijay is visibly upset.
Rosalie: I thought that was tomorrow...
Rosalie is puzzled.
Vijay: You're wrong. It was changed. I sent you an e-mail about it. This is all your fault.
Vijay is still annoyed.
Rosalie: Vijay, you're absolutely right. I apologize. I forgot to make the change in my agenda.
Rosalie is apologetic.
Vijay: You made it really difficult for me. If this project falls apart, I'm going to make sure everyone knows whose fault it is.
Vijay is now starting to calm down a bit.
Rosalie: So are you saying the clients might be unhappy because you did the presentation alone?
Vijay: No. I didn't do anything wrong. I did fine, considering I had no help from you, even though you were supposed to be there.
Rosalie: So everything went well with the clients. The issue is that I wasn't there to support you?
Vijay: Yes.
Vijay is now completely calm.

Rosalie realized she was at fault for missing the meeting with her clients. When Vijay confronted her about the issue, she dealt with his blaming behavior. In step one, Rosalie listened to what Vijay had to say. In step two, she showed understanding by stating the issue and owning up to her mistake.

Rosalie was successful in the first two steps because she was proactive in her approach. She was diplomatic and nonthreatening, and she used closed-ended questions to steer Vijay away from his blaming behavior. Rosalie has followed steps one and two for dealing with difficult people. Now it's time for step three – resolving the issue. Follow along as she deals with Vijay's blaming behavior.

Rosalie: I'm really glad you managed to handle things. Now let's talk about a solution to the issue. OK?

Vijay: Sure.

Rosalie: I want to prevent this from happening again. In the future, I'll make sure I put any schedule changes into my agenda immediately. I'll also give you my cell number so you can call me anytime. Is there anything that would help from your side of things?

Vijay: Well, I could use the automatic reminder feature on our in-house e-mail system. When you accept a tagged e-mail, I'll get a notification you've read it, and you'll get a series of reminders popping up on your computer screen until you acknowledge the change.

Rosalie: It sounds like we have a good solution. Thanks, Vijay. Well, I have to get back to my office. I'll see you at the team meeting tomorrow, and I promise you I'll be on time!

Vijay: I'll keep an eye out for you.

In the third step, Rosalie resolved the issue with Vijay by seeking a solution and then moving on. She was successful because she secured Vijay's trust and commitment by including him in a shared solution to the issue.

DEALING WITH A BLAMER

Dealing with a blamer

Now you'll have a chance to practice dealing with a blamer. You're an industrial designer for a company that designs and manufactures specialized sports equipment. You've just returned from representing your company at an international sports and fitness trade show. The event is very important for sales generation, as it's attended by all the major sports equipment wholesalers and retailers.

Unfortunately, your presentation of the company's new line of recyclable thermoplastic equipment wasn't a success. Many potential customers were lost because the prototypes were shipped to the wrong address and weren't available for the show. Focusing on blame is unproductive because it inhibits your ability to learn what's causing the issue and working on a solution.

CHAPTER 4. HOW TO WORK WITH MANIPULATIVE PEOPLE

CHAPTER 4. How to Work with Manipulative People
SECTION 1 - Types of Manipulative Behavior
SECTION 2 - Handling Manipulative Behavior
SECTION 3 - Dealing with a Manipulative Person

SECTION 1 - TYPES OF MANIPULATIVE BEHAVIOR

SECTION 1 - Types of Manipulative Behavior

There are four broad types of manipulative behaviors: trying to deceive, demonstrating inappropriate emotion, attacking on a personal level, and diverting attention. Before you can learn how to work with people who are manipulative, you have to be able to recognize their bad behaviors.

RECOGNIZING MANIPULATIVE PEOPLE

Recognizing manipulative people
Do you work with someone who is always meddling in everyone else's business? Maybe it's a nosy coworker who likes to interfere. Or maybe it's someone who instigates trouble, manipulating people and situations. Such people can be simply annoying, or they can even be spiteful and malicious.

Manipulative behaviors include threatening you, flattering you, making you feel guilty, or putting you down. Some manipulators display confusing behavior by alternating between being overly affectionate and charming and then being cold or angry. Manipulators thrive on getting others to unknowingly act out the manipulators' agenda. Being able to recognize manipulators in the workplace is vital to your career and your reputation.

Have you ever had to work with someone like this? Jose has a coworker who he thinks is stealing his ideas and taking credit for work he did. This coworker denies everything and tries to convince Jose that he's the crazy one. Jose is so angry and obsessed with the coworker's behavior that sometimes he wonders if it's true.

As Jose found out, manipulative people are generally subtle. When behaviors are hidden – as they are with most manipulators – you know something is wrong, but you can't pinpoint it. And, if you don't know what's really going on, it can make you feel as though you're the one at fault. So, being able to recognize manipulative people in the workplace is important for your emotional health.

Question

How do you think you could benefit by becoming more aware of the tactics manipulative people use?

Select possible benefits to being able to recognize manipulative behaviors.

Options:

1. You can be empowered
2. You can respond in an appropriate fashion
3. You can report manipulators to HR
4. You can use the same tactics against the manipulators

Answer:

Option 1: This is a correct option. Learning to recognize manipulative behavior can free you from a manipulator's control and empower you with a boost to your self-esteem.

Option 2: This is a correct option. Being able to recognize manipulators' moves will help you properly interpret their behavior and, therefore, respond appropriately.

Option 3: This is an incorrect option. Manipulative behavior is not usually a case for HR. In fact, many manipulators act innocent when confronted, and escalating the problem may do no good.

Option 4: This is an incorrect option. Being manipulative yourself will not help the situation and is not an appropriate response.

CATEGORIES OF MANIPULATIVE BEHAVIOR

Categories of manipulative behavior

Manipulative behavior isn't always easy to recognize, and manipulators don't often admit to their own controlling behavior. There are, however, some habitual behaviors that manipulative people engage in. Once you have a better understanding of these behaviors, you'll be able to recognize them and use strategies to deal with them.

Manipulators are driven to control things. They may be motivated by boredom in their personal or professional lives, or feel threatened by coworkers or their work situation.

Or they may simply be unhappy, since being petty and vindictive are often symptoms of insecurity or unhappiness.

However, manipulators may have good intentions – by meddling to try to help out – or they may be blatantly confrontational.

Some people manipulate from the sidelines, inciting you to get yourself in trouble. For example, Tanya wanted to take the lead on a software project for her boss, Bob. But Taku told Tanya he overheard Bob say he was giving that project to someone else.

In reality, all Taku overheard was Bob debating who to assign as project manager. But Taku wanted to see what would happen, so he exaggerated.

Tanya angrily confronted Bob because she felt she was being treated unfairly. She was penalized for jumping to conclusions, and Bob didn't appreciate being attacked. Taku incited the whole incident, but felt no repercussions.

Manipulators excel at controlling others. Their goal is to get you to do what they want, and they use many different tactics:

- withholding important information as a way of disempowering you,
- acting angry, or punishing you by shutting down and refusing to communicate,
- playing subtle mind games that keep you on your guard, and refusing to deal with conflict directly,
- making you feel guilty by acting ignored, forgotten, hurt, wounded, unloved, or uncared for,
- saying one thing and doing another, such as being pleasant to your face while talking viciously about you to others,
- pretending to be victims by acting helpless in situations where they are in fact the perpetrators of the problem, and
- promising a change in behavior, without having any intentions of actually doing so.

All the different tactics manipulators use can be grouped into four general areas. Types of manipulative behaviors include trying to deceive, demonstrating inappropriate emotion, attacking on a personal level, and diverting attention.

Trying to deceive

In addition to blatant lying, manipulators may try to deceive you by playing innocent, using outright denial, or playing dumb. For instance, when one manipulator was called to task, she said "I was just trying to help, how could I know you'd get in trouble?"

Demonstrating inappropriate emotion

Most people dislike confrontation and strong emotion, especially in the workplace. Manipulators use this dislike to get their own way by demonstrating inappropriate emotion. They may cry or pout, or get angry and either shout or give you the silent treatment.

Attacking on a personal level

Moving a dispute from a professional level into a personal attack is a common behavior of manipulators. The goal is to take the focus off them and to provoke you into an emotional, reactive response so you'll do what they want.

Diverting attention

To divert attention, manipulators downplay their behavior and try to convince people that the behavior is not as bad as it seems. Some common ways of doing this are by rationalizing, using guilt, playing the victim, and minimizing their actions. They divert blame to another person, change the subject, or divert the conversation when the topic is about their behavior.

The first behavior – trying to deceive – seems the most straightforward. But it's not always easy to tell when a person is lying. Sometimes you don't know you've been lied to until it's too late. Other times, the truth is clear when circumstances don't support the manipulator's story. But there are also subtle, covert ways to lie. Manipulators may lie by withholding some of the truth from you or by distorting it. They may be vague and leave out important facts, in effect lying by omission.

Manipulators may lie by flat-out denial, refusing to admit they've done anything wrong and playing innocent. Denial makes the victims feel unjustified. It's a maneuver used to make others back down or even feel guilty. Another way manipulators lie is by "playing dumb," or acting oblivious. This form of lying is exemplified by "I don't want to hear it" behavior. Using this tactic, manipulators can avoid paying attention to their controlling behaviors.

As an example of lying, consider Dominique's situation. Dominique is a project manager who has a manipulative coworker, Raj. She's trying to rally support for a new project initiative and asks Raj to get all those in favor together for a meeting. He deliberately leaves Enzo off the list – even though Raj knows he would be interested – because Raj doesn't like Enzo. Raj lies when he tells Dominique that Enzo isn't interested.

Question

Manipulative people try to deceive in different ways, including making a personal statement and pretending it's someone else's. This allows manipulators to put the blame on other people.

Which are statements people might use to try to deceive you?

Options:

1. "She thought you made a big deal out of the problem."
2. "Everyone thinks you should tell the boss what he said to you."
3. "I think John is right about the problem, don't you?"
4. "Amy asked me to meet with you about our next project task."

Answer:

Option 1: This is a correct option. Couching your opinion as someone else's is manipulative deception.

Option 2: This is a correct option. Making their opinions appear to be collective is one way manipulators try to deceive.

Option 3: This is an incorrect option. Expressing a personal opinion is being honest, not manipulative deception.

Option 4: This is an incorrect option. It's possible this statement is a lie, but it's not an example of making a personal statement and pretending it's someone else's.

The second category of manipulative behaviors is inappropriate emotional demonstrations. Examples of these outbursts include temper tantrums, tears, or displays of grief that are used habitually to manipulate other people. Temper tantrums are usually intended to intimidate you so that you will back off, and tears or grief are intended to make you refrain from upsetting the alleged victim even further.

The third category is one of the most emotional for any manipulator's victim – personal attacks. Personal attacks try to make the victim the cause of the issue. With this tactic, manipulators usually raise their voices and use aggressive "you" statements. They try to establish you as the root cause of any problems. If you play the manipulator's game, you end up in a fight without even knowing how it started.

Personal attacks are used to put you on the defensive. Using a combination of anger and guilt, many attacks begin with statements such as "Why do you always...", "Do you really expect me to...", "I can't believe you would...", or "How could you...". Remember Dominique and her coworker, Raj? Dominique found out that Raj hadn't invited Enzo to the meeting, even though he knew Enzo was interested in attending. Follow along as Dominique asks Raj about it.

Dominique: I ran into Enzo, and he was disappointed not to be included at the meeting.

Raj: Oh, that's completely unfair, he's totally out of line, as usual!

Raj says angrily.

Dominique: Now Raj, calm down. I know you don't really care for Enzo, but just let me finish.

Dominique says worriedly.

Raj: How dare you check up on my work behind my back? Why should I have to justify myself, when everyone knows you're the one in over her head with this initiative?

Raj says angrily.

Question

Which categories of manipulative behavior did Raj display?

Options:

1. Trying to deceive

2. Demonstrating inappropriate emotion
3. Attacking on a personal level
4. Standing up for himself
5. Withholding needed information

Answer:

Option 1: This is a correct option. Raj tried to deceive Dominique when he said "everyone knows" she's in over her head. He made a personal statement and pretended it was everyone's opinion.

Option 2: This is a correct option. Raj demonstrated inappropriate emotion by immediately getting furious when Dominique made a neutral statement about Enzo being disappointed.

Option 3: This is a correct option. Raj attacked Dominique personally by saying she was in over her head.

Option 4: This is an incorrect option. Standing up for yourself is not a manipulative behavior.

Option 5: This is an incorrect option. Withholding information is manipulative, but there's no indication that Raj is doing that.

The first three categories fit into the manipulators' need to do whatever is necessary to follow their own agenda. The last category – diverting attention – more often comes in to play after manipulative behavior is called out. Manipulators create diversions to try to downplay their behavior, and convince people the behavior is not as bad as it seems. Manipulators divert attention by blaming another person or by changing the subject.

Manipulators use distraction and diversion techniques to keep the focus off their behavior. Some common ways of diverting attention are by rationalizing, using guilt, playing the victim, and minimizing their actions.

Rationalization can be very effective for manipulators, especially when the explanation makes just enough sense that a reasonable person could accept it.

After all, if manipulators can convince you they're justified in their actions – or that their actions are no big deal – they can pursue their hidden agendas without interference. Playing the victim is a diversionary technique that manipulators use to gain sympathy and evoke compassion. The tactic is simple – convince someone that you're suffering, and they try to relieve your distress.

Attempting to evoke guilt ties in to the victim role, and usually refers to a shared history. Manipulators bring up previous actions and imply that you're uncaring, unfair, or ungrateful for not giving in to them now. The subtext of appeals to guilt is typically "Because I did this for you, you should do this for me now."

Examples of appeals to guilt

Manipulators will often appeal to guilt with statements such as:
- "Don't you care about me?"
- "If you liked me, you'd do it."
- "I thought we were friends."
- "Any decent person would help me out."

Follow along as coworkers Dominique and Raj further discuss Raj's slight against Enzo.

Dominique: Enzo is interested in the new project initiative. You should've invited him to the meeting even though you two don't get along.

Raj: Really? So you don't care that he insults me all the time? I would've thought that after I helped you last year, you'd stand by me. I guess I learned a hard lesson today.

Raj says sadly

Raj tried to divert attention from his actions by making Dominique feel guilty when he refers to a time in the past when he helped her. He also played the victim by trying to elicit sympathy about an alleged insult.

Question

You join a manufacturing company in a supervisory role, and Juan – one of your team members – resents that he didn't get your job.

Which examples display manipulative behavior?

Options:

1. Juan pretends he lost information you need due to his computer crashing

2. Juan gives you the silent treatment and refuses to communicate with you

3. Juan tells you that you're not smart enough or experienced enough to have the job

4. When you discuss the fact that Juan withheld information from you, he blames the IT crew and his computer

5. Juan downplays the time he helped you because he doesn't want everyone to know

6. Juan keeps a meeting's focus on fixing the crisis at hand instead of talking about his behavior

Answer:

Option 1: This is a correct option. If someone doesn't give you important information in hopes you'll appear less competent, he's manipulating you by trying to deceive you.

Option 2: This is a correct option. Juan is using inappropriate emotion to try to manipulate you.

Option 3: This is a correct option. Attacking you on a personal level is one way Juan tries to manipulate you into doing what he wants.

Option 4: This is a correct option. Blaming others is a way for Juan to try to divert attention from his own manipulative behavior.

Option 5: This is an incorrect option. Downplaying a positive action isn't a sign of manipulation. Juan may just be modest about what he did.

Option 6: This is an incorrect option. Juan might appear to be trying to divert attention, but in a crisis, his actions are justified and based in reality.

SECTION 2 - HANDLING MANIPULATIVE BEHAVIOR

SECTION 2 - Handling Manipulative Behavior

Knowing how to deal effectively with manipulative people at work will help you regain control and begin to enjoy your work environment again. It will also let you focus on work instead of on the manipulator, which helps you become more productive and effective. You'll gain the added benefit of being able to use the same coping skills in other areas of your life as well – manipulative behavior is not confined to the workplace.

There are five basic steps for handling manipulative behavior: meet privately, tactfully confront the manipulator, tell the person the behavior is unacceptable, outline your expectations for future behavior, and state the consequences of unchanged behavior.

BENEFITS OF HANDLING MANIPULATIVE PEOPLE

Benefits of handling manipulative people
Not knowing how to handle manipulative people at work can impact many areas. You may feel you have no control over your life, and there may be low morale in the workplace. Your energy and productivity are often spent on worrying about the manipulative people instead of on your work. All the wondering about what they'll do next can make you feel like you don't have the right coping skills to deal with their behavior. But it doesn't have to be that way.

Question
If not knowing how to handle manipulators can have such a strong impact, what do you think the benefits of being able to deal effectively with manipulative people in the workplace could be?

Options:
1. Better control over your work life
2. Increased morale
3. Increased productivity

4. Improve your coping skills for other areas of your life

5. Decrease the numbers of manipulators in your workplace

6. Better skills to out-manipulate other people

Answer:

Option 1: This is a correct choice. By learning how to deal with workplace manipulation, you'll regain a sense of control in your life. You won't have to feel pushed around by someone else's hidden agenda.

Option 2: This is a correct choice. By learning how to handle manipulative people, you won't dread going in to work. Enjoying your work environment again will raise your morale. And it just takes one person enjoying work to boost overall morale.

Option 3: This is a correct choice. By learning how to deal with manipulative people, you'll be able to focus more on your actual work. With fewer emotional distractions, you'll become more productive and effective at work.

Option 4: This is a correct choice. Being able to effectively handle manipulative people at work will give you coping skills you can use in other areas of your life. You may find coping skills especially useful in such traditionally high-stress personal negotiations as buying a house or car.

Option 5: This is an incorrect choice. Effectively handling manipulators won't eliminate them from your office, but you'll learn to deal with their behaviors.

Option 6: This is an incorrect choice. You don't have to become a manipulator yourself – nor would you want to – in order to deal with manipulative behavior.

DEALING WITH MANIPULATORS

Dealing with manipulators

Some people like being manipulators. They might try to instigate trouble, by doing things like spreading lies about coworkers to destroy their reputations, or they might simply play the victim to get sympathy or pawn off their own work. When acts of treachery and betrayal such as these are tolerated because the target of manipulation won't confront the manipulator, bad behavior is likely to escalate.

If manipulators are never confronted, they will continue to target people. Manipulative people thrive on controlling the emotions and actions of others. That's what gives them power. But if you can show them you won't be controlled, they'll lose some of that power. If you challenge their power, they may even stop the behavior on their own. But if you don't assert yourself and say no to manipulators, you're just another victim.

So, how can you confront a manipulator without setting yourself up for further attack? How can you convert such a person into an ally – or at least find a way to keep

yourself out of manipulative games? In general, when dealing with manipulative people, along with "don'ts," there are important "dos" to keep in mind:
- Do set healthy boundaries. You need to distance yourself emotionally in order to avoid getting caught up in the manipulative comments and behaviors. Cultivate detachment.
- Do document your interactions. These records can be useful later on in a confrontation or if you need to make a formal complaint about the manipulator's behavior.

Question

Master manipulators pride themselves in being able to get others to do their bidding. What are the "don'ts" when it comes to dealing with manipulators?

Options:

1. Don't let them know how they've made you feel
2. Don't ask them why they've done it
3. Don't hold your anger in
4. Don't get angry; just try to compromise

Answer:

Option 1: This is a correct option. Allowing manipulators to know your feelings will only enhance their sense of empowerment.

Option 2: This is a correct option. It's usually a waste of time to inquire why manipulators are behaving in a certain way. It's unlikely you'll get an honest answer, or even an answer that makes you feel better about their behavior.

Option 3: This is an incorrect option. It's pointless to get angry at manipulators. No matter how justified you may feel, it will only make you behave in the same negative fashion as the person you're upset with.

Option 4: This is an incorrect option. While it's true you shouldn't get angry, compromising with manipulators isn't a good idea. Compromise just encourages them to try to rework the conversation to get the outcome they want.

STEPS TO DEAL WITH MANIPULATIVE BEHAVIOR

Steps to deal with manipulative behavior
While these general dos and don'ts are good to keep in mind, there are also five specific steps you can take to deal with a manipulator. When you decide to confront someone who is trying to manipulate you, first make sure you meet privately. Second, gently confront the person, and then, as the third step, explain that the behavior is unacceptable. Fourth, outline your expectations for future behavior, and finally, state the consequences if those expectations aren't met.

The first step is to meet privately to discuss the matter. A positive outcome to the confrontation is more likely if you don't humiliate the person by discussing it in public. Try to find a private but somewhat informal or neutral environment. Non-neutral environments include standing in front of a large group of people or, if you are the person's manager, sitting across from your desk.

You should speak calmly when you ask to see your coworker. For example, you might say, "I need to talk to you about a problem. Do you have a few minutes? We could meet in the planning room, which is free right now."

Question

Where do you think would be an appropriate place to have a discussion with your manipulative coworker?

Options:

1. At the person's desk, which is surrounded by other cubicles
2. In a conference room or an unused office
3. In your home or the person's home
4. At a restaurant

Answer:

Option 1: This is an incorrect option. Meeting somewhere surrounded by other cubicles isn't private. If you talk to manipulative people in public, they may become more defensive or aggressive. Speaking about the issue in this environment could also make the surrounding employees uncomfortable.

Option 2: This is the correct option. A meeting in a conference room or in an unused office would be private and neutral, since it's not your "home turf" nor the other person's.

Option 3: This is an incorrect option. A meeting at your home or the person's home would be private, but inappropriate for a work discussion and not neutral ground.

Option 4: This is an incorrect option. While a restaurant is neutral ground, it's neither private nor an appropriate place for a serious workplace discussion.

Once you and the manipulator get to a private area, the second step is to gently confront the person. If you stay silent, you implicitly condone the manipulator's behavior. Confronting manipulators lets them know you're not an easy mark. And making the other person aware that you know what's going on is often enough to stop the manipulation. Either way, the manipulator's power is reduced.

In a confrontation, you need to be calm and not let your emotions show. In a soft tone of voice, clearly explain the problem to your coworker.

Don't get pulled into arguing. Listen to what your coworker says, but then leave the situation alone. You may have to agree to disagree, since manipulators will usually try to convince you their actions are justified.

Consider the example of Rosa and Raymond, who work in a software company on the same project team. Raymond has evidence that Rosa is withholding important information from him. She seems to enjoy the trouble this manipulation causes within their team, as well as between their team and other departments. After Raymond asks Rosa to meet with him privately, he gently confronts her about her behavior.

Follow along with Rosa and Raymond's conversation.

Raymond: Rosa, you said you gave my assistant that report I needed, but I never got it. Later on, I saw it sitting on your desk.

Raymond sounds calm.

Rosa: Really? Well, maybe your assistant forgot it.

Rosa says, innocently.

Raymond: When I don't get the information I need from you, I miss my deadlines. This is a problem for our team and for the people waiting for our work. Was it your intention to withhold information from me?

Raymond says, calmly.
Rosa: Of course not!
Rosa sounds unhappy.

Raymond tactfully confronted Rosa when he clearly stated the problem. He didn't get drawn into an argument or get defensive when Rosa tried to shift the blame. He remained calm while telling Rosa the impact of her behavior, and made it clear he understood her motivation when he asked about her intentions.

Question

Suppose a close friend at work says she overheard another coworker telling your manager that you shouldn't be the team lead because you're not qualified. You've had problems in the past with this other coworker, so you ask to meet with him in private.

Which examples exhibit an appropriate approach to confronting such a manipulator?

Options:

1. "As I understand it, you told the boss I wasn't qualified to head up the new team. Is that true?"

2. "I know you're aware of my qualifications. Is it your intent to try to keep me from getting the team lead position?"

3. "You know I'm qualified. Saying otherwise makes me feel like you're out to get me."

4. "How could you do such a thing? I thought we were friends."

Answer:

Option 1: This is a correct option. Stating the issue calmly and clearly is the right way to begin a confrontation with a manipulator.

Working with Difficult People

Option 2: This is a correct option. Asking the manipulator what his intentions are is the appropriate way to continue confronting the person.

Option 3: This is an incorrect option. Stating your feelings will only put the focus on you and not on the manipulator's actions. Manipulators will usually jump at the chance to divert attention from their behavior.

Option 4: This is an incorrect option. Using guilt will only put you on the same level as the manipulator. You need to state the issue clearly, and then ask the other person about his intentions.

After you've stated issues clearly and asked about the manipulator's intentions, wait for a response – the next move is the other person's. After this, the third step is explaining that the behavior is unacceptable. The manipulator may not intend to cause problems – or, at least, may not admit to such intentions – but either way, you need to make it clear that such behavior is not acceptable.

The most common responses you'll get to your questions about intentions will be excuses, arguments, and accusations. Manipulators try to divert attention and minimize the situation. If the manipulator denies wanting to cause trouble – as often happens – you can put the person on notice without forcing an admission by saying "That's good, because I can't tolerate that."

If the manipulator does admit to causing the problem, you can then ask why. Either way, the third step in dealing with manipulative behaviors is to tell the person the behavior is not OK. Once you've made it clear that the manipulative behavior is unacceptable, the fourth step is to outline your expectations for future behavior. Clearly define what behavior you want to see in the future. This includes asking the manipulator to do what you asked. Ask about the other person's level of commitment to changing the behavior. For example, you should ask something like, "Can I count on this behavior stopping?"

Regardless of whether the manipulator answers yes or no about committing to change – or even if the person agrees with you or not – the last step is to state the consequences if the behavior doesn't change. Some manipulators will exhibit strong reluctance to committing to change. Or they will continue to argue with you about it, even in the late stages of your discussion. Consequences will depend on the situation, of course, but could include bringing the issue up with the boss, asking for mediation from HR, or getting corroborative documentation to the appropriate people.

Question

You're dealing with a manipulative coworker who tries to take credit for your ideas. You've told her that this behavior is unacceptable and has to stop.

Which is the best example of how to state the consequences of unchanged behavior to the manipulator?

Options:

1. "If you don't stop taking credit for my work, I'll copy everyone on the e-mails so they'll be clear about who came up with which idea."

2. "You better stop stealing my ideas, or I'll tell the boss and get you fired."

3. "You told the boss that my idea for the new design was yours. Did you intend to take the credit for my work?"

Answer:

Option 1: This is the correct option. A clear consequence for not changing manipulative behavior in this case might be to include everyone on the e-mail distribution list so credit is appropriately given.

Option 2: This is an incorrect option. Threatening the other person might just escalate any manipulative behavior.

Option 3: This is an incorrect option. Gently stating the problem and asking about the manipulator's intentions is an example of how to confront the behavior, not how to state the consequences.

In a hospital, two nurses – Jenna and Akira – are vying for position as head nurse. Jenna has been badmouthing Akira to the hospital administrator, Ramon. Jenna told Ramon that Akira was late on several occasions. Although Akira hadn't had a chance to check in on those days, Jenna knew full well that Akira was in the hospital working on emergencies.

Akira asks Jenna to meet her in the surgical supply room, which is one of the few private areas available for a discussion. Follow along as Akira talks to Jenna about the situation.

Akira: Jenna, I know you've told Ramon some things about me being late for work that aren't quite true. What are you trying to accomplish by this?

Akira says, calmly.

Jenna: Nothing. We were just talking and the subject of lateness came up. Jenna says, defensively.

Jenna says, defensively.

Akira: Well, you don't even have your facts straight. I've never been late, and you badmouthing me to the administrator isn't behavior I can tolerate.

Akira says, calmly.

Jenna: I don't think I did anything wrong, and you were late. Jenna says, petulantly.

Jenna says, petulantly.

Akira: If you had asked me about it, I'd have told you that I was here working on emergencies before I got a chance to sign in. Talking about other people behind their backs is wrong. In the future, please don't do it. If you have a problem with me, talk to me first. Will you do that?

Akira remains calm.

Jenna: I can do that. Jenna says, reluctantly.

Jenna says, reluctantly.

Akira: That's good. If it happens again, I'll be forced to go to HR with all my documentation. They need to know what is and isn't true.

Akira says, with determination.

Akira handled the discussion with Jenna very well. She said what she was thinking, but she did it without threatening Jenna. First, she chose a private place to have the talk, which isn't easy in a busy hospital. Then she confronted Jenna about the problem by simply stating it, bringing the behavior out in the open. Akira explained to Jenna that badmouthing other people is unacceptable.

She then outlined her expectation that Jenna would stop her manipulative behavior, and stated the consequences – delivering proof to HR – if the behavior continued. Akira followed the five steps, and did it in a way that wouldn't negatively impact her working relationship with Jenna.

Question

Working with Difficult People

You work with someone who's trying to manipulate you by withholding information from you. Sequence the steps to take to handle manipulative behavior in this scenario.

Options:

A. Invite the manipulator to talk with you in an unused office

B. Calmly state the problem, and ask about the manipulator's intentions

C. Let the person know you won't tolerate the behavior

D. Tell the person you expect the behavior to stop

E. Let the person know what you plan to do if the behavior continues

Answer:

Invite the manipulator to talk with you in an unused office is ranked as the first step. Inviting someone to discuss the issue in an empty office is an example of meeting privately – the first step in handling manipulative behavior.

Calmly state the problem, and ask about the manipulator's intentions is ranked as the second step. Stating the problem and asking about intentions is an example of gently confronting the person – the second step in handling manipulative behavior.

Let the person know you won't tolerate the behavior is ranked as the third step. Letting the person know the behavior is intolerable is an example of telling the person the behavior is unacceptable – the third step.

Tell the person you expect the behavior to stop is ranked as the fourth step. Telling the person you expect the behavior to stop is an example of outlining your expectations for future behavior – the fourth step in handling manipulative behavior.

Sorin Dumitrascu

Let the person know what you plan to do if the behavior continues is ranked as the fifth step. Telling the person what you'll do is stating a consequence for the behavior not changing. This exemplifies the fifth and final step of handling manipulative behavior.

SECTION 3 - DEALING WITH A MANIPULATIVE PERSON

SECTION 3 - Dealing with a Manipulative Person

Trying to work with manipulative people can be exhausting. To stop getting caught up in their schemes, you need to shut down their machinations and empower yourself. To accomplish this, you need to apply the five strategies: meet privately, gently confront the manipulator, tell the person the behavior is unacceptable, outline your expectations for future behavior, and state the consequences if the behavior doesn't change.

DEALING WITH MANIPULATIVE BEHAVIOR

Dealing with manipulative behavior
Sometimes, it may seem like everyone wants something from you. Maybe your boss wants you to work longer hours, or your coworker wants you to ignore his poor work. Salespeople want you to buy something, and customers need your time. When you say yes, is it your choice, or is it because you were manipulated into it?

Throughout life, you'll encounter people who are controlling and manipulative. But you don't have to feel frustrated or powerless. You can regain control of your energy and time when you use the five basic steps to deal with a manipulative person. First, meet privately with the manipulator, then gently confront the person. Tell the person the behavior is unacceptable, outline your expectations for future behavior, and state what the consequences will be if the behavior doesn't change.

Manipulation may be attempted through a person trying to deceive you, demonstrating inappropriate emotion, attacking you on a personal level, or trying to divert attention. Many manipulators try to use guilt to get people to do what they want.

Consider the situation Amrit is in. She works for an energy company as an accountant. One of her coworkers, Enrique, has recently had a hard time keeping up with his work. Although they've never been particularly close, Enrique cornered Amrit one afternoon and told her all about his wife, who's recuperating from major surgery.

Then Enrique asked Amrit for what he described as a "favor." He wants her to finish up his accounts so he can go home early, and for her not to tell the boss about it. Enrique tells her he feels his personal circumstances warrant her help. He says he'd do the same for her. Amrit is flustered by the request and asks him for a little time to think about it.

After going back to her desk and thinking, Amrit realizes that if Enrique really needed the time off, he could go to the boss and ask for it through normal channels. She realizes he's trying to manipulate her into doing his work, and decides to confront him. Amrit goes to Enrique's cubicle and says "What you're asking just isn't right, and we need to talk about it."

Question

Did Amrit correctly carry out the first step in dealing with manipulative behavior?

Options:

1. Yes
2. No

Answer:

The first step in dealing with manipulative behavior is to meet privately. Enrique's cubicle is not private, nor is it a neutral area.

Enrique agrees to talk to Amrit, but only if they go to an unused office where they can close the door. Follow along as Amrit talks to Enrique.

Amrit: Enrique, you seem to be trying to get me to do some of your work. Is that what you mean to do?

Amrit asks calmly.

Enrique: Well, I'm just trying to go home to my sick wife. I would think most people would be glad to help out in a situation like this.

Enrique says sadly.

Amrit: If you need to go home, you know you just have to talk to the boss. I do have sympathy for your situation, but using my feelings to try to get me to take over your work is just not acceptable.

Amrit says calmly.

Enrique: You know the boss isn't easy to talk to. I thought you'd help out. Enrique whines.

Amrit: I'll do it this time, but you really should have gone through proper channels.

Amrit says with some irritation.

Enrique: Thank you!

Enrique exclaims smugly.

Question

Which steps in dealing with manipulative behavior did Amrit complete successfully?

Options:

1. Gently confront the person
2. Tell the person the behavior is unacceptable
3. Outline your expectations
4. State the consequences

Answer:

Working with Difficult People

Option 1: This is a correct option. Amrit gently confronted Enrique when she stated the problem and asked him what his intentions were by saying "Enrique, you seem to be trying to get me to do some of your work. Is that what you mean to do?"

Option 2: This is a correct option. Amrit clearly told Enrique that his behavior was unacceptable when she said "I do have sympathy for your situation, but using my feelings to try to get me to take over your work is just not acceptable."

Option 3: This is an incorrect option. Amrit did not outline any expectations for future behavior. She told Enrique "I'll do it this time, but you really should have gone through proper channels." She did not tell him to talk to the boss before she'd help, either for this instance or in the future.

Option 4: This is an incorrect option. Amrit did not state any consequence for Enrique's behavior not changing. She may be hoping that once his wife is better this kind of situation will no longer arise, but manipulators don't usually stop.

To effectively deal with Enrique's manipulative behavior, Amrit still needs to outline her expectations for the future. She could tell him "Of course I'll help you out whenever I can. But you have to talk to the boss first. Will you agree to that?" Then, whether he states his agreement or not, Amrit should tell Enrique what will happen if he tries to guilt her into covering for him again. She could simply say "If you don't go to the boss first, I will."

CHAPTER 5. HOW TO WORK WITH SELF-SERVING PEOPLE

CHAPTER 5. How to Work with Self-serving People
　SECTION 1 - Dealing with Arrogant People
　SECTION 2 - Dealing with Busybodies
　SECTION 3 - Dealing with Self-serving People at Work

SECTION 1 - DEALING WITH ARROGANT PEOPLE

SECTION 1 - Dealing with Arrogant People

Arrogant people are a fact of life. But once you understand that the root of their arrogant behavior is a basic fear of rejection, you can learn to deal with them. In addition to generally refusing to lose your cool and engage in an angry debate, there are three distinct steps you can apply to help neutralize the impact of an arrogant person. You can ask for an explanation of the behavior, express your disapproval, and then move on.

RECOGNIZING ARROGANT BEHAVIOR

Recognizing arrogant behavior

"Wow. I bet you never thought someone from your social background would ever have a job this good." This sort of simultaneous boast and put-down is a hallmark of arrogant behavior. Arrogant people make

statements, ask questions, and give you looks that manage to make you feel small and insignificant. They can make your work life miserable. Learning to deal with this type of person will make you feel better about yourself, allow you to be more productive, and make going to work a pleasure instead of a chore.

How confident people behave

Confident people often empower others, because they feel comfortable with themselves and are completely secure. Confident people don't waste time constantly trying to impress you, and they don't try to overpower others or make them feel stupid.

In contrast to the behaviors of confident people you may have identified, arrogant people tend to be insecure. They're afraid that you'll expose them as the frauds they are. Arrogant people try to position themselves above everyone else because fear of rejection is the foundation of their behavior. This fear of rejection causes them to overcompensate and motivates them to exaggerate their own worth in an overbearing way.

Arrogant people's feelings of insecurity may not even be warranted. They may in fact be as good or better at what they do than everybody else. But they aren't sure of that and so they overcompensate. Rather than focusing on improving themselves, arrogant people concentrate on diminishing others. Arrogant people try to diminish others by showing disrespect through sighs, looks, tone, or the way questions are phrased. They always seem to be asking, "Why?" in a belittling manner. They may roll their eyes, make sarcastic observations, or make jokes at others' expense.

As a result of their insecurity, arrogant people crave attention. In discussions, they show off by doing a lot of talking and not much listening. They have little interest in what others have to say, so they often interrupt when other people are speaking. They tend to overpower other speakers, question the purpose of decisions, and dismiss ideas other than their own. Arrogant people tend to ask questions in such a way as to imply that the other person's knowledge, performance, or thinking is inadequate.

Marko is the chairman of a city budget committee that includes Nils and Bernice. Bernice is known for being arrogant. Follow along with the committee's deliberations to observe Bernice's behavior.

Nils: As you'll all notice in the proposal, I've suggested a new program for remodeling and updating all city buildings in the next five years.

Bernice: Great idea. And I suppose you're going to pay for that out of your own pocket?

Bernice says sarcastically.

Marko: How exactly would you fund that kind of initiative Nils? Nils: Well, I have a few different ideas.

Nils says hesitantly.

Bernice: And I'll bet not one of them will actually cover the total cost, right ?

Nils: Uh, well...no. But with a few cuts elsewhere, we might be able to cover the expense.

Bernice: I thought so...

Bernice says triumphantly.

Question

In the preceding scenario, did Bernice display arrogant behavior?

Options:

1. Yes. Bernice focused on diminishing Nils.
2. No. Bernice's approach was assertive and reasonable.

Answer:

Bernice displays arrogant behavior by trying to diminish Nils. Her comments make him seem like he came to the table with a half-finished proposal that has no chance of success. By trying to make Nils look bad, Bernice hopes to appear more knowledgeable.

Arrogant people often try to build themselves up by bragging. They like to lord their status, knowledge, money, and resources over you. Bragging may be done in an indirect way. As arrogant people complain about particular troubles – troubles which are naturally much more impressive than yours – they may slip in a little bragging.

Working with Difficult People

For example, have you ever heard someone say something like "I really love my luxury sports car, but you wouldn't believe how much effort it takes to maintain"? Clearly, that person is not really asking for sympathy but rather is trying to impress you. Arrogant people constantly talk about their problems, speaking for the sake of sensationalism, and are always playing the victim. They compare every situation someone relates to them with something they've experienced. By measuring someone else's experiences against their own seemingly far more important stories or difficulties, they diminish the other person.

Question

Which actions or statements exemplify arrogant behavior?

Options:

1. Someone refocusing the discussion on a similar experience from her own past where she successfully handled a much bigger issue with far fewer resources.

2. Saying "Did you see the size of my new office? I don't know how I'll ever use all that space."

3. Saying "I've done this kind of thing before. I'd be glad to coach you on some of the techniques if you'd like."

4. Someone who says, "I've got a degree in engineering so I should be able to review the technical specifications for you."

5. A person continually interrupting others in a discussion to point out that, in his experience, the point they're discussing will never be an issue.

Answer:

Option 1: This is a correct option. Much like their tendency to brag, arrogant people often compare what is said to their own situations to make their problems seem greater or their experiences seem more interesting.

Option 2: This is a correct option. Arrogant people try to set themselves above you by bragging about their abilities or their situations.

Option 3: This is an incorrect option. This is not an arrogant statement. Arrogant people don't try to empower others, whereas this person is confident and willing to share knowledge.

Option 4: This is an incorrect option. The statement displays confidence rather than arrogance. The person is not attempting to diminish you in any way.

Option 5: This is a correct option. Arrogant people tend to overpower others when they try to make a point, often interrupting to relate their own experiences, which they consider more important.

TECHNIQUES FOR HANDLING ARROGANT PEOPLE

Techniques for handling arrogant people
Arrogant people aren't likely to just go away. They need attention, and need to demonstrate their superiority over you in order to bolster their own confidence. You won't be able to ignore them, so you might as well deal with them and improve your time at work. If you could deal with their behaviors using a few simple steps, wouldn't that be time well spent?

There are some general do's and don'ts to consider when dealing with arrogant people. Do be confident. If you know your own self-worth, believe in your abilities, and feel you are strong, intelligent, and valuable, arrogant people can't diminish you. Their ability to belittle you is determined by one person – you.

Your strongest asset when dealing with arrogant people is your confidence. Stay true to yourself. Don't rise to the bait when an arrogant person tries to get to you. Giving in to the temptation to react to their put-downs and off-handed insults gives them exactly what they want – power over you. Instead, remain calm. In addition to the things you should do, there are some things you should not do with an arrogant person.

Don't argue. Getting into a debate with an arrogant person is a no-win situation. You can't win because arrogant people really aren't interested in listening to what you have to say. While you are busy arguing the facts, they will be using sarcasm, derision, and every other tool in their arsenal to make you insecure in your point of view.

Don't get angry. Getting angry and losing control is what arrogant people want you to do. Once you've lost control of yourself, they're in control of the situation.

You can and should make the effort to deal with arrogant people affecting your work life and end their influence over you. A basic open-and-close approach to arrogant behavior uses three simple steps:

1. open up the discussion by immediately confronting the arrogant person about the behavior using an open-ended question,
2. state your disapproval of the arrogant behavior, and
3. close the door on the conversation by moving on to other business, giving the arrogant person no chance to respond.

The first step, using an open-ended question to confront, puts the arrogant person in the position of having to defend insulting or belittling behavior. Instead of using closed-ended questions, which can be answered quite simply, you might ask "What exactly did you mean by that?" or "Why are you rolling your eyes?" These questions require the person to explain in more detail.

After asking an open-ended question, make sure to wait for a response.

Question

You're discussing your work schedules with a coworker. Every time you bring up having to work on weekends, he immediately tells you he always works weekends, and that he works harder than anyone else in the department.

What's the most appropriate way to confront him about his arrogant behavior?

Options:

1. "Why are you acting like your extra work is more important than mine?"

2. "Are you saying that your work is more important than mine?"

3. "Your work is no more important than mine, you know."

Answer:

Option 1: This is the correct option. Asking why your colleague is talking about himself is an open- ended question that makes him explain his arrogant behavior.

Option 2: This is an incorrect option. Asking a closed-ended question such as this will get you a yes or no answer. Your colleague will not have to explain himself.

Option 3: This is an incorrect option. Making a confrontational statement like this just escalates the problem. Unless you ask an open-ended question, your coworker will not be required to explain his arrogant behavior.

Arrogant behavior is difficult and embarrassing to explain. When confronted, an arrogant person may try to backpedal and claim what was said was just a joke. Or the person may press on and attack further. Either way, it's awkward and difficult to paint oneself as a reasonable person after being insulting or rude.

The second step is to state your disapproval briefly and directly. Say something like "I don't think making fun of my suggestion is appropriate." You should also outline your expectations for future behavior such as "I'd like us to get through this meeting without further sarcasm." Doing this restores your control of the situation.

The final step is simply to move on. Don't engage in further debate. By employing the first two steps, you've effectively neutralized the behavior. There's nothing to gain and everything to lose by continuing to discuss it.

Remember the budget committee meeting where Bernice arrogantly put down Nils' proposal for updating all city buildings? She sarcastically asked if Nils was going to pay for it himself and derided his suggestions as inadequate. Fortunately, Nils is a fairly confident person who understands how to use the three steps for dealing with arrogant behavior.

Follow along with the committee's deliberations to learn how Nils applied the appropriate steps for dealing with Bernice.

Bernice: I think it's dumb to even pursue this line of inquiry without a viable funding plan. Are we supposed to just wave our magic wand?

Nils: Bernice, what exactly do you expect to achieve with sarcasm and insults?

Bernice: Uh, I wasn't being insulting. I was just kidding around. I do think that the plan is kind of dumb, I mean...I don't exactly understand how you think it can work.

Nils: I don't think sarcasm is called for, and I'd appreciate it if you could refrain from calling my ideas "dumb."

Bernice: Well...sorry.

Bernice says sheepishly.

Nils: Let's just get back to discussing the budget proposals. We have a lot of serious work to do here.

Nils dealt effectively with Bernice's arrogant behavior. He applied the three steps by first asking her to explain her behavior with an open-ended question. As Bernice dismissed his concern as a joke and continued to press her attack, Nils expressed his disapproval, stating his expectation for future behavior in the meeting.

When Bernice tried to discuss the issue further, Nils moved on, which helped negate Bernice's influence and take away her control of the situation.

Question

How do you think you would benefit by being able to effectively deal with arrogant people?

Options:

1. You'll feel better about yourself
2. You'll enjoy a higher level of productivity
3. You will have a sense of accomplishment
4. You'll be able to avoid future conflicts with the arrogant person
5. Arrogant people will respect you and avoid being overbearing in your presence

Answer:

Option 1: This is a correct option. Benefits of coping with the arrogant people in your workplace include feeling like a valued employee, having a better attitude, and feeling good about your working environment.

Option 2: This is a correct option. When you worry about coping with an arrogant person, you spend less time focusing on tasks. By learning to cope, you'll free up your time and energies for your work.

Option 3: This is a correct option. Dealing with an arrogant coworker isn't easy. Doing so effectively will make you feel like you've really accomplished something, and you'll feel like the time involved was well spent.

Option 4: This is an incorrect option. You won't be able to avoid conflict, but you can reduce the effects of arrogant behavior by learning how to deal with it.

Option 5: This is an incorrect option. Arrogant people are motivated by fear of rejection. Their need to diminish you in order to elevate themselves won't decrease as you learn to deal with their behavior.

Question

Liam is an accountant at a small firm. One of the other accountants, Harriet, is always bragging about her big clients and her connections. During a meeting one day, she made fun of several of Liam's clients, saying how their accounts must be easy to maintain because they are so small.

Match the steps for dealing with arrogant behavior to the corresponding actions Liam could take to address Harriet and her jokes. Not all actions will match to a step.

Options:
A. Confront
B. Disapprove
C. Move on

Targets:
1. Liam asks Harriett what she meant by her comment.

2. Liam tells Harriet that insulting each other's clients is unacceptable, and he expects she will stop making jokes at his expense.

3. Before Harriet can comment further, Liam redirects the discussion back to the current tax problems.

4. Liam acts assertively, standing up for his clients.

5. Liam says sarcastically, "Well, at least I'm on time with all my paperwork. You're always late. I guess it must be all those 'big' clients of yours, huh?"

Answer:

This is a correct option. The first step in addressing Harriet's arrogant behavior is to ask her an open-ended question that requires her to explain herself.

This is a correct option. Liam expresses his disapproval and his future expectations. This is the second step of the open-and-close method for dealing with arrogant people.

This is a correct option. The final step Liam applies for dealing with arrogant behavior is to simply move on without giving Harriet any further opportunity to justify her behavior or press the issue.

This is an incorrect option. Although acting assertively is generally good, it's not one of the steps to effectively address Harriet's arrogant behavior. She's not interested in Liam or his clients except to the degree that she can diminish him in order to elevate herself.

This is an incorrect option. Responding sarcastically does not correspond to one of the steps. Liam should avoid rising to bait and stay calm in the face of Harriet's arrogant behavior.

SECTION 2 - DEALING WITH BUSYBODIES

SECTION 2 - Dealing with Busybodies

Busybodies dig up information that they have no right to and then spread it around via the improper channels of gossip and rumor. To deal with the busybodies in your office, you can begin by refusing to participate as either a gossiper or a listener. When ignoring the gossip isn't enough and you need a strategy for dealing with a specific busybody issue, there are four key steps to take: ask for the busybody's reasoning; disapprove of the behavior; suggest talking to the subject of the gossip; and remind the busybody of the potential consequences.

IDENTIFYING BUSYBODIES

Identifying busybodies

Miguel is the resident gossip at the small software company where he works. Recently, a few curious requests for information crossed his desk, and he started thinking. He decided they might indicate an upcoming merger with one of the company's competitors. The other day in conversation, he related his supposedly inside knowledge to one of his coworkers, exaggerating a bit along the way. By the end of the day, the entire office was in an uproar. Rumors were flying, people were upset, and arguments were breaking out.

The results of Miguel's rumor mongering included lost productivity, wasted time, low morale, hurt feelings, divisiveness, and increased anxiety among employees. He was in line for a promotion, but now Miguel's chances for advancement aren't looking good. His boss found out he started the rumor and she no longer trusts him with information. She thinks he's unprofessional and can't understand why he would do it. Why was he compelled to stick his nose in everyone else's business? The answer is simple. Miguel is a busybody.

Busybodies are the office gossips. Their primary goal in life seems to be uncovering information no one else has and passing it on. Busybodies need to feel important, and they get that feeling when they appear to know things before anyone else does.

In the course of spreading rumors, busybodies often betray confidences and discuss sensitive information. That's not surprising – that's just the sort of inside information they believe will enhance their image in certain people's eyes. No secret is safe when a busybody is around. For that reason – and many more, including their effects on morale and productivity – you need to learn to identify the busybodies in your workplace and become skilled at dealing with them.

If someone begins a statement by saying, "I really shouldn't be telling you this, but...", then chances are you've found your workplace busybody. And, with an opening like that, it can be tempting to join in by listening further and engaging in gossip yourself. But remember, a busybody is unlikely to keep a confidence, so anything you say to that person will probably soon be public knowledge. And do you really want to be seen as a gossip yourself?

You may have correctly noted that busybodies often have low self-esteem. Spreading rumors and seeming knowledgeable makes them feel more important. People who engage in workplace gossip may also do it because they believe it will help them "fit in." They think sharing behind-the-scenes information with others will make them part of the group. Sadly, gossiping often has the opposite effect, instead lowering people's opinion of the gossiper.

Working with Difficult People

Busybodies aren't simply people who talk about others. They actively pry into knowledge areas that are not their business. Busybodies dig up information and then present it to others in such a way that it makes them appear smarter for having known it.

Unlike legitimate distributors of information, busybodies don't use proper channels for spreading around what they know. They can't, because they aren't supposed to be privy to the information in the first place. So to get the word out, they use the informal methods of gossip and rumor.

Consider the case of Martha and Boris. Boris often finds out early about new initiatives and changes to office policy by hanging out with Martha, the chief operating officer's assistant. Martha sends out all the company policy memos, so she knows a lot. As she sends out each e-mail memo, she's always glad to take a few minutes and explain any confusing language or complex procedures.

Boris passes on what he learns from Martha, being careful to never mention her name. Everyone in his department thinks Boris is really on the ball. They often go to him with questions about things they've heard through the grapevine, and he always seems to have inside information on what's happening.

But recently, Boris's coworkers discovered that he'd misinformed them. He'd speculated that the company was soon going to be converting to a new filing system. The chief operating officer is upset because people think there's a big change coming, despite his assurances to the contrary. He's asking around to determine the source of the rumor. Someone is going to be in trouble for being a busybody, but who should it be?

Question

In the case of Boris and Martha and the false rumor of a system changeover, who should the department head consider the busybody?

Options:
1. Boris
2. Martha

Answer:

Option 1: This is a correct option. Boris is the busybody. He's the one who's claimed knowledge of something that isn't his business and spread information to make himself feel more important.

Option 2: This is an incorrect option. Martha is not the busybody. She disseminates information through legitimate channels and only adds clarifying information as she informs the rest of the company.

Question

One of your coworkers, Justine, is in the habit of gossiping to other people at work.

Which of Justine's actions and behaviors indicate she is a busybody?

Options:

1. Justine says she found someone in the tech support department who says the company is planning to change graphics software in the coming year, but she can't tell you who it is

2. At lunch, Justine confides her suspicions to her friends about what changes will result from the new software

3. Justine researches the software she thinks will be chosen and sends everyone she knows copies of the online manual

4. Justine often interrupts when others are trying to make their opinions known
Answer:
Option 1: This is a correct option. Justine's behavior is indicative of a busybody because she actively pries into areas that are not her business and she claims to have inside information.

Option 2: This is a correct option. Justine is spreading rumors rather than facts, and she is doing so through informal channels. This is busybody behavior.

Option 3: This is an incorrect option. By passing around the manual, Justine is just sending out potentially useful information through proper channels.

Option 4: This is an incorrect option. Interrupting others is a sign of arrogance. It's not typically indicative of a busybody.

TECHNIQUES FOR DEALING WITH BUSYBODIES

Techniques for dealing with busybodies

There are some general tips that can help you deal with busybody behavior. These tips all fall under one general idea – "don't play the game." You can begin to address busybody behavior by limiting your involvement with the people you identify as busybodies. You can't trust them not to reveal your secrets, so why would you want to associate with them any more than you have to?

Think about it. Do you really want to be known as the person who hangs around with the office gossip? It's very easy to get drawn into the gossip habit and it can be hard to resist the lure of having inside information. But you can discourage busybody behavior by refusing to participate. Don't let yourself spread gossip. Communication is a two-way street, and so is gossip. Busybodies can't exist without an audience, so deny them one. Don't listen to gossip.

Let your coworkers know directly that you aren't interested in participating in gossip. You don't have to be judgmental – just say that you're not comfortable with the idea. For example, you could say, "I don't like talking about things when I don't have all the facts" and then excuse yourself from the conversation. Walking away from a gossip situation sends the message to everyone involved that spreading rumors is not acceptable. Others may even follow your example.

When you have to address a specific problem with a busybody, there are four basic steps to follow:

1. ask the busybody why they think the information should be spread around the office,

2. let the busybody know that you're uncomfortable with the gossip,

3. suggest to the busybody that you both go and talk to the person who's being gossiped about - the subject of the gossip, and

4. remind the busybody of the consequences of workplace gossip.

Step 1: Ask why

Start by confronting the busybody and asking why the person thinks the information in question should be spread around and why it's appropriate for that person to do so. There's no excuse for betraying confidences and sticking your nose where it doesn't belong, so the busybody will probably have difficulty trying to explain the reasoning behind the act.

Step 2: Disapprove

The second step is to express your disapproval, regardless of whether or not the busybody tries to defend the behavior. Let the busybody know you don't approve of disseminating private or sensitive information.

Step 3: Suggest talking to subject of gossip

In the third step, you can drive home the point about the inappropriateness of the behavior by suggesting that you both go speak to the subject of the rumor and see what that person thinks. It's unlikely that the busybody will take you up on this suggestion.

Step 4: Remind of consequences

As a final step, remind the busybody there are consequences for spreading gossip and rumors. If your workplace has a specific policy regarding the spreading of gossip and confidential information, point that out to the busybody.

Nico is the assistant to the president of a bank. One of her colleagues, Hans, is the office gossip. He's always fishing for information about things that aren't related to his job. Recently, he started a rumor that the loans department would be downsizing by 20% in the next quarter. Nico doesn't know where Hans got this idea, and as far as she knows, it's groundless. But, true or false, she decides to deal with it before morale is affected.

Follow along as Nico uses the four steps to deal with Hans and his busybody behavior.

Nico: So Hans, Jenny tells me that you're the source of the information that's going around about the loan department downsizing. Is that true?

Hans: That's right. I hear it's going to be about 20%.

Nico: Well, I have no real knowledge either way, but I'm pretty sure the executive board didn't confide in you and ask you to spread information like this. Why are you getting everyone upset with your speculation? Are you trying to scare everyone into looking for new jobs?

Working with Difficult People

Hans: Well, no. I just heard about some meetings that were taking place on the subject and put two and two together. I think people want to know about these things.

Nico: I don't think spreading your speculations around as if they were facts is right. As assistants, we're expected to be discrete.

Question
How well did Nico executed the first two steps for addressing busybody behavior?

Options:
1. Nico executed both steps well
2. Nico successfully executed one step
3. Nico failed to execute any of the steps

Answer:
Nico effectively executed the first two steps for dealing with a busybody. She asked Hans for the reasoning behind his behavior and then she directly expressed her disapproval.

Follow along with the conversation as Nico continues to confront Hans about his busybody behavior using the final two steps.

Nico: People will naturally assume this information came from your boss. Let's go ask her if it's OK to be talking about this. Maybe she can provide some clarification on the company's future plans.

Hans: Ah...well, let's not. She wouldn't be too happy about it. Hans says nervously.

Nico: All right. But keep in mind the memo the president circulated last month on confidential information. I think it applies to this sort of gossip. If he knew about this, you'd probably be officially reprimanded.

Hans: I see what you mean.

Nico effectively applied the four steps for dealing with a busybody. She confronted Hans about his gossiping and asked why he thought he was right to be spreading rumors. Nico followed that with an expression of her disapproval and a suggestion that they bring the issue out into the open. She suggested asking the person most affected by the gossip, in this case Hans's boss, to weigh in.

Finally, she gently reminded Hans that their company has a documented policy on the subject of workplace confidentiality and his behavior could have official consequences.

Question

Manny and Victoria work in the same department of an electronics retailer. Victoria has been gossiping about a colleague, Gamba, who is taking night courses to get his MBA. Victoria has told everyone Gamba is planning on quitting as soon as he graduates because another company has offered him a position. Manny decides to confront Victoria about her gossiping.

Match the steps for dealing with a busybody to examples of their correct application. Not all examples will have a match.

Options:

A. Step 1: Ask why

B. Step 2: Disapprove

C. Step 3: Suggest talking to subject of gossip

D. Step 4: Remind about consequences

Targets:

1. Manny asks Victoria why she considers it OK to spread rumors about private matters

2. When Victoria responds defensively, Manny says discussing someone's personal business is wrong

3. Manny suggests he and Victoria go ask Gamba about his plans to settle the matter

4. Manny points out to Victoria that the company considers rumor-mongering a form of harassment

5. Manny explains his reasoning on why Victoria shouldn't spread rumors

Answer:

Asking Victoria an open-ended question regarding her rationale for spreading rumors matches to step one, ask why.

Manny employs the second step when he disapproves of spreading rumors about personal matters.

Suggesting they approach the victim of Victoria's busybody behavior aligns with step three, suggest talking to the subject of the gossip.

Gently reminding Victoria about company policy is a way to execute step four, reminding the busybody about the consequences of their behavior.

Manny explaining his reasoning doesn't match to any step. In the second step, Manny should simply express disapproval.

x

SECTION 3 - DEALING WITH SELF-SERVING PEOPLE AT WORK

SECTION 3 - Dealing with Self-serving People at Work

Busybodies and arrogant people are two types of self-serving people that can be difficult to work with. There are effective techniques to address each type of behavior. If, for example, you identify someone as displaying arrogant behavior, you can apply the three steps to manage it: confronting them, disapproving of the behavior, and quickly moving on to avoid further discussion.

If, instead, the person displays the characteristics of a busybody, you can use a four-step process to try to change the person's behavior. You can ask for the person's reasoning, indicate your disapproval, suggest talking to the subject of the gossip, and remind the person about potential consequences.

ADDRESSING SELF-SERVING BEHAVIOR

Addressing self-serving behavior
People use a variety of behaviors to get what they want. Although self-serving people come in many forms, two common types – arrogant people and busybodies – can be dealt with effectively if you use the appropriate strategies. First, you need to recognize which type of behavior you are dealing with, and then apply the correct steps.
Question
Arrogant people and busybodies have different characteristics and display different behaviors. Match examples of types of self-serving behaviors to the appropriate category of self-serving people.
Options:
A. Lonnie does most of the talking and very little listening in discussions, and often sighs and looks away as others speak

B. Peter pries into areas that aren't his concern to get information he can use to appear more knowledgeable and important

C. Arlo compares every situation he's told about with his own problems and past experiences, often playing up his victim status

D. Juno thinks discussing inside information will help her fit in with coworkers

Targets:
1. Busybodies
2. Arrogant people

Answer:
Busybodies are people who pry into knowledge areas that are not their concern and share inside information to make themselves appear more important or to help them fit in.

Arrogant people are likely to compare every situation someone relates to them with their own experiences and problems. They tend to talk a lot and listen very little as they are uninterested in what others have to say. They may show disrespect and try to diminish others by sighing or looking away when someone else is speaking.

Consider the case of Paulo and Jameeka. They are on the same committee charged with developing the corporate goals for the coming year. Paulo came into the latest meeting with an aggressive attitude. He had already decided on the four primary goals he would agree to. After presenting his ideas, Paulo pushes for a vote. But the committee chairman suggests they put off voting until more ideas are presented.

As other members chime in with their proposed goals, Paulo often interrupts and shoots holes in their proposals in a derisive way. Even when he isn't talking, he's rolling his eyes, sighing, and generally indicating through his body language his total disregard for what everyone else has to say.

At the end of the meeting, Jameeka is frustrated and angry at Paulo, and at herself. Instead of standing up for her ideas, she held back her comments and withdrew from the discussion for fear of ridicule. As the meeting ends, Jameeka tries to address Paulo's behavior. She walks right up to him and lets him know what she's feeling. Follow along with their conversation to learn how Jameeka deals with Paulo.

Jameeka: Paulo, your behavior was demeaning toward everyone and my feelings were hurt.

Paulo: Well, I'm sorry, but all I did was present another side to the argument.

Jameeka: You ridiculed each idea presented. After a while, most people who wanted to speak up and put ideas forth, didn't – including me.

Paulo: If your ideas are so good, they should stand up under pressure. I think it's better that the weaker ideas don't get put forth.

Jameeka: That's no way to encourage creativity. In the future, could you try being a little more encouraging and less derisive?

Paulo: I don't really see the need.

Paulo says dismissively.

Jameeka: You really are an arrogant jerk!

Jameeka says angrily.

Question

Jameeka's attempts to get Paulo to listen to reason failed miserably because she didn't correctly apply the three steps to help neutralize his arrogant behavior. Sequence the steps as you would have applied them to the preceding situation.

Options:

A. Ask Paulo why he thinks interrupting and disparaging other people's ideas is okay

B. Tell Paulo you don't approve of rudeness and narrow-mindedness, and let him know you expect him to be open to other people's ideas at future meetings

C. Say "See you at the next meeting"

Answer:

Ask Paulo why he thinks interrupting and disparaging other people's ideas is okay is ranked the first step. Your first step is to calmly confront the arrogant person about the behavior with an open-ended question and wait for a response. This puts him in the awkward position of having to justify his rudeness.

Tell Paulo you don't approve of rudeness and narrow-mindedness, and let him know you expect him to be open to other people's ideas at future meetings is ranked the second step. Your second step is to briefly and directly state your disapproval of Paulo's arrogant behavior and include your expectations that future behavior will improve.

Say "See you at the next meeting" is ranked the third step. You effectively employ the final step by immediately moving on after showing disapproval. Saying "See you at the next meeting" takes away any chance Paulo might have had to debate the issue further.

But busybodies can be stopped by appropriate use of the four steps: asking for the person's reasoning, indicating your disapproval, suggesting talking to the subject, and reminding the person about potential consequences.

When you apply the steps correctly, you can help Kylie examine – and hopefully change – her negative behavior.

CHAPTER 6. DEALING WITH MICROMANAGERS

CHAPTER 6. Dealing with Micromanagers
SECTION 1 - Dealing with a Micromanager
SECTION 2 - Practice: Dealing with a Micromanager

SECTION 1 - DEALING WITH A MICROMANAGER

SECTION 1 - Dealing with a Micromanager

Micromanagers can be difficult to work with, and they aren't likely to change much, if at all. Consistently using a four-step process will help build the micromanager's confidence in you. With confidence will come trust in your ability, and the micromanager is likely to back off and let you work more independently.

The steps of the process are to lay out your plan of action ahead of time to the micromanager, make any required changes to your plan, be dependable, and update the micromanager frequently. Learning to deal with the micromanagers you encounter at work will reduce the negative impact they have on you.

RECOGNIZING MICROMANAGERS

Recognizing micromanagers
Lily walks into your office and asks to know what your plan of attack is for a task you've been assigned. This is the second time she's been in today to find out how you're progressing. Before she leaves, she asks if you can provide an update before you go home. Is Lily a micromanager? The answer is partly influenced by Lily's relationship to you. If Lily is your manager and you're working on a task that requires a lot of support, perhaps she's just doing her job. But if Lily is your coworker, then she could very well be trying to micromanage your work.

It can be difficult and uncomfortable to work with someone who wants to micromanage your tasks. The best approach is to preempt the behavior – plan for it, and be prepared to deal with the micromanager before the behavior starts. But before you can do that, you have to be able to recognize a micromanager.

Three indicators can help you determine whether your coworker is a micromanager. If the person tells you precisely how to do your work, expects updates more often than is productive, and presents a bottleneck to overall performance, you may be working with a micromanager. Suppose you have a colleague who's constantly looking over your shoulder and telling you how to do your work – the first indicator of a micromanager. What do you suppose drives that behavior? For that colleague, it's likely all about control. In an effort to maintain a sense of control, micromanagers will tell you exactly what you need to do, when you need to have it done, and how you should do it.

Consider Todd and Giselle, who work together. Even though they've both been assigned separate tasks, Todd keeps involving himself in Giselle's work. Giselle is getting frustrated. She feels as though Todd doesn't trust her to do her job – he's constantly giving her direction about how to do her work and telling her when she should have it done. Right now they're planning a silent auction – the organization's annual, charity fundraiser. Giselle has organized it for the last five years. This is Todd's first year. He's in charge of soliciting auction donations.

Follow along for an example of the micromanaging behavior Giselle routinely experiences when she works with Todd.

Todd: Giselle, please tell me you booked the venue for the silent auction.

Giselle: Yes, I booked it last year. The day after the auction, actually.

Todd: Oh, OK. Good thinking Giselle. I'd sure like to see you get the promotional work started. It would be a shame if the success of the auction was negatively impacted by a lack of timely promotion.

Giselle: I agree. That's why I've planned the promotional strategy and delegated tasks to experienced colleagues. We meet twice a week to make sure things are getting done as planned. You're welcome to join us, if you like.

Giselle says, pleasantly yet a little disgusted.

Todd: Perfect, I think I'll do that. One last thing, Have you applied for the permit to sell liquor? I'd like that to be done by March 30th.

Giselle: Actually Todd, I plan to have that done by the end of this month because you need to apply a minimum of 45 days before the event. Otherwise you can't get the license.

The second indicator that a coworker is a micromanager is that the person expects updates more often than is productive. It's very frustrating when you find yourself doing more updating than actual work. Remember Giselle? She's frustrated by Todd's continual requests for updates. The time she spends satisfying Todd's "need to know" is putting her behind schedule. She doesn't know how much more she can take without saying something she might regret.

Follow along to learn how Todd's requests for updates are affecting Giselle's work on the silent auction preparations.

Todd: Giselle, I thought I'd drop in to see how you made out changing the meal options. We talked about this yesterday and I haven't heard anything.

Giselle: Todd, I've taken care of the menu. I just didn't have time to let you know. I've been concentrating on doing the paper work for the liquor permit – it needs to be sent in today. This takes priority over giving you updates.

Todd: Well, all you have to do is send a quick e-mail. I just want to make sure the auction is a success. Perhaps you need to work on your time management skills.

Giselle: Really! Well maybe if you didn't ask for updates on everything I do, I'd have the time to do my work! In the last day you've asked for updates on three of my tasks. I think you've been in my office almost as much as I have. You need to back off.

The third indicator that you're dealing with a micromanager is when that person presents a bottleneck to performance. Such is the case with Todd and Giselle's team. On Monday morning, the team is meeting to discuss progress and projections for the week. Unfortunately, this week's progress reports aren't good. Many projects – Giselle's included – are behind schedule because they're awaiting Todd's input, which he's insisted is necessary. Todd's micromanaging has created a bottleneck that impacts his and the team's productivity.

A micromanager can easily become overburdened and have a hard time keeping up with all the extra, unnecessary work. Unfortunately, it's the overall productivity and performance of the organization that's affected, not just that of the micromanager.

Question

Which examples indicate that the coworker in the situation is a micromanager?

Options:

1. Aimee has provided you with detailed step-by-step instructions on how to perform a task you've done many times before

2. Leo has just walked into your office for the second time this morning to find out where you are with your work

3. Your team has just missed a deadline because of Joe's insistence on being involved in everyone's work and his demands for frequent updates

4. On behalf of the project manager, Kiley distributes a schedule for achieving project deadlines, and dates are included for all team members

5. June has created a very detailed plan to guide her team through a task they're unfamiliar with

Answer:

Option 1: This option is correct. Being told how to do your work in detail by a coworker who is equal to you in authority is a sign that the coworker is micromanaging you. Learning to deal with micromanaging behavior will allow you to work more independently.

Option 2: This option is correct. Micromanagers need to know everything, including how you are progressing. If you learn to effectively deal with micromanagers, you can greatly reduce the amount of unnecessary reporting you have to do.

Option 3: This option is correct. Missing deadlines is never a good thing. Micromanagers like Joe can become a bottleneck, slowing down a team's progress. Learning to effectively deal with micromanagement can improve overall productivity.

Option 4: This option is incorrect. Kiley is just acting on behalf of a superior. She is not attempting to micromanage her coworkers.

Option 5: This option is incorrect. Sometimes it's necessary to create detailed plans. It's not an automatic indicator of micromanagement.

DEALING APPROPRIATELY WITH MICROMANAGERS

Dealing appropriately with micromanagers

The two most common reasons that individuals micromanage are inexperience and a lack of confidence in the abilities of others. Because micromanagement creates challenges to productivity, you need to work to build up the micromanager's confidence in you.

Individuals who are experienced in their roles may micromanage as a way of maintaining control. On the other hand, the uncertainty that comes with performing new or unfamiliar tasks can intensify a micromanager's need to be in control. However, micromanagement is likely to subside as the individual gains experience. One way to address a micromanager's lack of confidence is to build the person's trust in you. Essentially, micromanagers don't trust others to do a good job. This absence of trust and need to be in control combine to produce this lack of confidence.

Question

Working with Difficult People

Which of these areas do you think you can influence to reduce the micromanaging of your work by coworkers?

Options:

1. Experience
2. Confidence

Answer:

Option 1: This option is incorrect. You have no control over your coworkers' experience level. Only they can increase their level of experience. If you're dependable, their trust in you and confidence in your ability to do your job will grow too.

Option 2: This is the correct option. You can help build your coworkers' confidence in you by being dependable and proving you can do your job.

If you find yourself working with a micromanager, you can take some specific steps, in sequence, to build that individual's confidence in you: lay out your plan of action ahead of time to the micromanager; make any required changes to your plan; be dependable, and; update the micromanager frequently.

Step one is to lay out your plan of action ahead of time to the micromanager. This helps to demonstrate that you know what you're doing, that you're in control, and that you're paying attention to detail. Emulating the working style of the micromanager can give that person a sense of comfort and can help build trust and confidence.

Consider breaking your work into logical milestone deliverables that indicate how you'll get from the beginning of your work to the successful completion. Pay attention to detail, and include information about what, how, and when.

When you approach the micromanager, you may want to explain that, by developing this plan of action, you hope to ensure that you share a common understanding of what must be done. Or maybe mention that you value this person's input, explaining that, since your work together is contributing to one overall outcome, it's important to cooperate.

Consider this example of two coworkers, Amelia and Charles. Working with Charles is difficult because he's a micromanager. Amelia decides to change her approach to working with him. The first thing she does is create a detailed plan of the work she needs to do. Once it's finished, Amelia e-mails him the plan. She's included milestones, as well as a step-by-step description of how she'll do the work. She extends an invitation to review the plan with Charles after he's had a chance to review it.

Question

Suppose you're working with a micromanaging coworker, Kerry, and you want to try adjusting your approach to see if you can minimize her micromanagement of you and your work. What is the first thing you should do?

Options:

1. You should develop a detailed plan outlining what, how, and when you intend to do your work

2. Present Kerry with your plan and have her review it

3. Request Kerry provide you with details of what she expects from you

4. Meet with Kerry and establish ground rules for her involvement in your work

Answer:

Option 1: This option is correct. Developing a plan that details your work will help preemptively answer Kerry's questions.

Option 2: This option is correct. Presenting Kerry with your plan and asking for her input will help resolve concerns she has with the plan before you start your work.

Option 3: This option is incorrect. You shouldn't give Kerry this much control. To build trust and confidence, you need to demonstrate you can do the work.

Option 4: This option is incorrect. This tactic is unlikely to work with Kerry. You're better off changing your approach than trying to change hers.

Step two is to make any required changes to your plan. Work with your micromanaging coworker until this person is satisfied that your plan is workable and detailed enough that you'll accomplish what needs to be done. How you proceed with this step will depend on if an agreement is reached or if an agreement isn't reached upon presentation of your action plan.

If agreement is reached

If agreement is reached, you can move forward with your work.

If agreement isn't reached

If agreement isn't reached, you need to make the changes necessary to gain agreement. You may want to ask how your coworker measures success or what the person's expectations are, and then incorporate that input into your plan. Again, move ahead with your work only once you achieve agreement on the what, how, and when details of your work.

After reviewing Amelia's plan, Charles has some concerns. The two meet to discuss the plan and make some changes. Amelia feels it's sufficient to generate a computer model of the new device. However, Charles would prefer it if she developed a working prototype. Even though she thinks this is unnecessary, it won't take that much time and will appease Charles. She also agrees to add details about how the prototype will be used, when, and by whom. Once these changes are made, Charles agrees the plan is sufficient.

Benefits of reaching an agreement

Securing an agreement on how you'll accomplish what needs to be done before you begin working can reduce interference by your micromanaging coworker. Micromanagers are less likely to change what they've already agreed to, which means fewer changes and fewer interruptions. One resulting benefit of this is the ability to work more independently and productively. Another benefit is that the direction and detail provided in the plan will help avoid unnecessary reporting.

Question

Suppose your micromanaging coworker, Kerry, has just finished reviewing your plan of action. What should you do next to appropriately deal with her micromanagement?

Options:

1. Ask Kerry if she has any input to your plan

2. Make any changes suggested by Kerry

3. Move ahead with your work while you wait for Kerry's input

4. Tell Kerry to consult the plan, not you, with concerns

Answer:

Working with Difficult People

Option 1: This option is correct. Asking Kerry for input will help identify any concerns that, if left unresolved, may increase her micromanagement of you.

Option 2: This option is correct. Once Kerry agrees to your plan, she's less likely to want to make changes as you work. Making the changes she requests before you start working will help minimize her micromanagement of you.

Option 3: This option is incorrect. You need to resolve any concerns Kerry has with your plan of action before you begin to work. Agreement to the plan will help minimize the micromanagement you experience throughout the project.

Option 4: This option is incorrect. The action plan is not intended or expected to stop Kerry from consulting with you as you work. But it should reduce her interruptions because she's agreed to what you plan to do.

Step three is to be dependable. Conduct the work as agreed – essentially, do what you've said you'd do. This will help you to build a trusting relationship with your micromanaging coworker. Always fulfill the commitments you made in your plan of action. Failing to do so will ruin your efforts to build the micromanager's trust in you. When the micromanager trusts you, the person will likely interfere less, and feel less of a need to try to control everything you do.

Now that Amelia is completing her work, she's taking care to stick to the plan that her and Charles agreed to. And she notices that Charles is not looking over her shoulder as often as he used to. She figures there's merit in changing her work habits to suit Charles's micromanaging ways. She's able to get her work done with minimal interruption from Charles, and she's no longer frustrated.

Question

As you work with Kerry, your micromanaging coworker, what can you do to help build her confidence in your abilities?

Options:

1. Do the work as agreed to in the action plan
2. Consistently deliver on promises that you and Kerry agreed to
3. Ask Kerry to help you to demonstrate your abilities
4. Ask Kerry how you can gain her confidence

Answer:

Option 1: This option is correct. Kerry will become more confident in your abilities as you deliver on what you said you would.

Option 2: This option is correct. You need to keep all your mutually agreed on promises. Letting her down on anything the two of you agreed to will damage your efforts to gain her confidence and trust.

Option 3: This option is incorrect. Asking Kerry to help you just to demonstrate your abilities wastes your time and hers. Instead, focus on doing what you agreed you would.

Option 4: This option is incorrect. Asking Kerry how you can gain her confidence wouldn't do much to actually build it, even if she did tell you. You build confidence by doing what you said you would in your action plan.

Step four of the process for appropriately dealing with micromanagers is to update the micromanager frequently. Providing frequent progress reports – perhaps even daily – satisfies a micromanager's "need to know" and reduces the number of times the micromanager comes to you for updates. This helps control and minimize the interruptions, which provides the benefit of improved overall productivity.

Amelia is about to leave work for the day. She's recently made it a habit to drop by Charles's office at the end of each workday to tell him what's going on with her work. She has found this to be an effective way of keeping Charles from interrupting her.

Question

As you work with your micromanaging coworker Kerry, what can you do to minimize her tendency to interrupt you as you work?

Options:

1. Provide Kerry with updates often
2. Provide Kerry with updates without being asked
3. Ask for Kerry's input frequently
4. Provide Kerry with input often

Answer:

Option 1: This option is correct. Providing updates often will satisfy Kerry's micromanaging need to know and can reduce her need to check up on you.

Option 2: This option is correct. Voluntarily providing updates before Kerry asks can help build her trust in you and her confidence in your abilities.

Option 3: This option is incorrect. You won't need to ask Kerry for her input, nor will you likely want to. Typically, micromanagers will provide more input than is necessary.

Option 4: This option is incorrect. Spending time providing input on Kerry's work will take you away from your own. This runs counter to your overall objective of being more productive.

By following the four-step process, Amelia has found that Charles is micromanaging her less. She's getting more done and isn't as frustrated as she was the last time she worked with him. Amelia intends to use this process each time she needs to work with Charles. She believes that being dependable and working to accommodate Charles will help build his confidence in her. And their working relationship will continue to improve, allowing her to be more productive and less stressed.

Consistently following this four-step procedure will help you build a relationship based on trust. The micromanager will notice that you're dependable and will have confidence in your abilities. In turn, this should minimize the micromanaging you're subjected to. If this doesn't work, you may need to seek outside help. Your manager or supervisor is probably the most appropriate person to start with. Your immediate superiors are most likely to be familiar with the circumstances and individuals involved. You also want to avoid upsetting the chain of command.

Question

What are the benefits of learning to deal with micromanaging coworkers?

Options:

1. Working more independently
2. Avoiding unnecessary reporting
3. Improving overall productivity
4. Eliminating extra reporting
5. Avoiding unnecessary interruptions

Answer:

Option 1: This option is correct. The ability to work more independently is a benefit of learning to deal with micromanagers. Try giving them what they need to feel in control without allowing them to be controlling.

Option 2: This option is correct. Try volunteering information. This will give micromanagers the detailed information they want, but on your time.

Option 3: This option is correct. Often times micromanagers will present a bottleneck to productivity, but you can lessen this tendency by learning to properly deal with their behavior.

Option 4: This option is incorrect. Micromanagers will always seek more information than is necessary to do their jobs, and therefore extra reporting will be required. However, supplying information before you're asked for it can reduce the number of reports requested.

Option 5: This option is incorrect. You're likely to continue to be unnecessarily interrupted by your micromanaging coworker, but the frequency should diminish as the individual gains confidence in your abilities.

If necessary, you can consider other potential sources of help outside your department:
- human resources,
- the micromanager's supervisor or manager, if different from yours, and
- the company's employee assistance program, if it has one.

Before seeking help, compile your evidence. Make sure you have proof that the micromanager's behavior is negatively impacting your performance. If applicable and available, you can also include information about how the micromanager's behavior is negatively impacting project or team efforts. Evidence gives weight to your argument and provides a better basis for action – you want to avoid being seen as pointing fingers and passing blame.

Question

Keisha and Ormond are working on a project together and Keisha needs to deal with his micromanaging ways. Access the learning aid Keisha and Ormond to learn more about the situation.

Based on the scenario, which aspects of dealing with her micromanaging coworker, Ormond, did Keisha handle appropriately?

Options:

1. Lay out your plan of action ahead of time to the micromanager
2. Make any required changes to your plan
3. Be dependable
4. Update the micromanager frequently

Answer:

Option 1: This option is incorrect. Keisha didn't think it was necessary to perform this step because she knew what she was doing. Unfortunately, this won't cut it with a micromanaging coworker. Laying out a plan can help reduce a micromanager's anxiety about not being in control.

Option 2: This option is correct. Once Keisha decided to develop a detailed plan of action, she also asked for Ormond's input. As a result, he'll be less likely to ask for changes, since he's already agreed to her plan.

Option 3: This option is correct. After agreeing to the plan, Keisha made sure she stuck to it. This helped build Ormond's confidence in Keisha's abilities. It also builds his trust that she'll do what she says, freeing her to do her job more independently.

Option 4: This option is incorrect. Keisha didn't provide frequent updates. If Keisha had provided frequent updates, it would have helped to build Ormond's confidence in her and reduced the number of updates wanted, allowing Keisha to work with fewer interruptions.

SECTION 2 - DEALING WITH A MICROMANAGER

SECTION 3 - Dealing with a Micromanager

Micromanagers are unlikely to change their ways completely, but you can alleviate the level of micromanagement you're subjected to by working to suit the micromanager's needs. Consistently following a four-step process that includes laying out your plan of action ahead of time to the micromanager, making any required changes to your plan, being dependable, and updating the micromanager frequently can help.

REVIEWING THE PROCESS

Reviewing the process
Once you're comfortable in understanding the steps to deal with a micromanaging coworker, you'll be better equipped to put them into action. In turn, you'll be able to work more independently, keep reporting requirements reasonable, and improve your productivity. Building a good working relationship with a micromanager requires you to establish trust and build the coworker's confidence in your abilities. Consistently following the four-step process for dealing with micromanagers can help you do this.

Jasper and Caroline are working together on a project to create an in-house certification study guide. Jasper knows that Caroline tends to micromanage her coworkers. He decides to be proactive and change his approach to suit her needs and hopefully lessen her micromanagement of him. Before doing any project work, Jasper creates a detailed plan of what he'll do, and how and when he'll do it. Jasper has finished his plan and is about to present it to

Caroline for her review. Follow along as Jasper talks to Caroline about his plan.

Jasper: Caroline, I've outlined my contributions to this project and I'd like you to take a look before I start working. Since my work will impact yours, I thought it would be a good idea for us to be on the same page.

Caroline: Great, Jasper. Let's have a look. Your work spans the entire project.

Jasper: Yes. I'm in charge of creating the style sheet, editing, assuring quality, and ensuring final acceptance of the study guide. I've also included details of what I'll do, how, and when for each of my project tasks. Can you think of anything I missed, or do you have any input to improve on my plan?

Caroline: Well, I think you'd be better off doing a complete editorial review, instead of doing a section at a time. That way, you can catch any contradictions from section to section.

Jasper: You mean wait until the study guide is written and then do one editorial review instead of smaller reviews as the guide is completed? Sure, I can do that. Anything else?

Caroline: No, the rest looks good to me. I can't wait to see how things progress.

Jasper: Ok, so I'll make that change and add the necessary details. Once I'm done, I'll e-mail you a finalized copy of the plan. Thanks for your input, Caroline.

Knowing that micromanagers need information, Jasper provides frequent updates on his progress. And knowing that Caroline will be watching him closely, Jasper is careful to follow the plan exactly. Caroline has even complimented him on his attention to detail and ability to deliver. He knows this will help build Caroline's trust and confidence in him. Jasper sends Caroline updates whenever an established milestone is reached. But he also e-mails Caroline daily updates, just to keep her well informed.

REFERENCES

References
1. **Managing Difficult People: A Survival Guide for Handling Any Employee** - 2004, Marilyn Pincus, Adams Media
2. **Working with Difficult People, Second Edition** - 2009, Michael S. Dobson, William Lundin, and Kathleen Lundin
3. **How to deal with a passive-aggressive perso**n - Colette Georgii, Helium
4. **Managing Workplace Negativity** - 2001, Gary S. Topchik
5. **Dealing with Difficult People, Third Edition** - 2006, Roy Lilley, Kogan Page
6. **Warriors, Workers, Whiners, and Weasels: Understanding and Using the Four Personality Types to Your Advantage** - 2006, Tim O'Leary, Xephor
7. **Disagreements, Disputes, and All-Out War: 3 Simple Steps for Dealing with Any Kind of Conflict** - 2008, Gini Graham Scott

8. **How to Easily Handle Difficult People Handbook: Everything Problem-People Don't Want You to Know** - 2006, Oxman, Murray, Sourcebooks
9. **The Disgruntled Employee: Manage Challenging Staff without Losing Your Mind** - 2008, Morris, Peter, Adams Media
10.

GLOSSARY

Glossary
A
arrogant behavior - Behavior that tries to belittle others in order to elevate oneself. Arrogant people give the impression that they consider themselves to be better than everyone else when, in fact, they are basically insecure.

authority - The power or right to give orders and instructions and to make decisions.

B
blaming - Making statements that attribute fault or accountability for a negative outcome to some other person or situation.

busybody - An individual who seeks out information beyond the scope of his responsibilities and spreads it to others for the purpose of seeming more knowledgeable and powerful.

C
closed-ended question - A question phrased to elicit a short dichotomous response.

complaining - Expressing feelings of pain, dissatisfaction, or resentment, usually directed toward a specific person, object, or situation.

coworker - A person working with another worker, usually at or near a similar level of authority or responsibility in the workplace hierarchy.

F

feedback - Information communicated to an individual, work unit, or team about job-related performance or behavior.

H

hostile aggressive - An individual who uses intimidation and anger to get what he wants. A hostile-aggressive person tends to be resentful, offensive, belligerent, and a bad listener.

hothead - A hostile-aggressive personality type prone to sudden outbursts of anger and rage. Anger is triggered when the individual perceives a physical or psychological threat. Anger is likely to be followed by fear and suspicion.

I

initiative - An organizational program, project, or effort that has a specific purpose, goals, and objectives. See project.

K

knowledge warden - A passive-aggressive person who refuses to part with information in his control.

M

micromanager - An individual who asserts control by involving himself in the details of his work and the work of others.

N

negativity - Habitual conduct involving the tendency to resist or express skepticism toward positive or constructive behavior.

O

open-ended question - A question phrased to elicit a full meaningful response. An open-ended question may be phrased as a question or as a statement that implicitly requires a response.

P

passive aggressive - An individual who uses manipulation and secrecy to get what he wants. A passive-aggressive person typically comes across as quiet, shy, always nice, never defensive, and unassertive.

positive reinforcement - Specific praise or rewards targeted at a subject with the purpose of increasing the future frequency of a desired behavior.

procrastination - Behavior characterized by the deferment of actions, tasks, or decisions to a later time.

project - A collaborative enterprise with a defined beginning and end that is planned to achieve particular goals and objectives.

R

rapport - Harmonious accord between two people.

resistance - Noncompliant behavior.

U

unresponsive aggressor - A passive-aggressive type who appears uninterested in communicating and may fail to respond to questions.

V

verbal assailant - A hostile-aggressive personality type who tends to attack with words. Verbal assailants are openly abusive, abrupt, intimidating, and overwhelming.

They generally pick an aspect of an individual's behavior or personality to attack.

W

waffler - A passive-aggressive type who hates to make decisions, always wants to be on the winning side, and desperately wants the approval of others.

whining - Uttering unfocused, self-pitying statements with the purpose of soliciting sympathy or attention.

www.ingramcontent.com/pod-product-compliance
Lightning Source LLC
Chambersburg PA
CBHW020907180526
45163CB00007B/2652